AN INTRODUCTION
TO JAPAN

AN INTRODUCTION
TO JAPAN

by Herschel Webb

under the direction of

HUGH BORTON

DIRECTOR, EAST ASIAN INSTITUTE, COLUMBIA UNIVERSITY

and

DOUGLAS W. OVERTON

EXECUTIVE DIRECTOR, JAPAN SOCIETY

COLUMBIA UNIVERSITY PRESS

New York 1955

This book has been sponsored by the Japan Society, a private, nonprofit, nonpolitical association of Americans and Japanese who desire to help bring the peoples of the United States and Japan closer together in their appreciation and understanding of each other and each other's way of life. Offices of the Society are located at the Savoy-Plaza, Fifth Avenue at 58th Street, New York 22, N.Y.

PREFACE

An Introduction to Japan has been prepared and published under the auspices of the Japan Society in an effort to meet a growing interest in Japan and Japanese-American relationships on the part of American colleges, schools, and adult education groups. In a sense the present volume is the successor to the *Japan Society Syllabus*, last published in 1937. Rather than prepare a new edition of the *Syllabus*, however, the editors have felt it desirable to begin afresh and to issue a completely new volume, which would not only reflect the great changes that have taken place in Japan in the intervening years but also take into account the fundamental alteration in the relationship between Japan and the United States from one of rivalry between two mutually distrustful powers to the far more complex interdependent relationship of today.

Readings and films listed at the end of each section are merely suggestions and are not intended to comprise an exhaustive bibliography. For further materials the reader is referred to the best short bibliography on Japan, *A Selected List of Books and Articles on Japan in English, French, and German,* revised and enlarged edition, compiled by Hugh Borton, Serge Elisséeff, William W. Lockwood, and John C. Pelzel, Harvard University Press, 1954.

The author wishes to acknowledge the courteous assistance

given him by Miss Miwa Kai and Mr. Philip Yampolsky of the East Asiatic Library, Columbia University, and Mrs. Mildred Ostler of the Lincoln (Nebraska) Public Library. Among others who read the manuscript, particular thanks are due to Nadine Murayama and Katharine Wells for the many excellent suggestions they made while this work was in progress.

The cover design and chapter decorations are the work of Charles M. Saito.

December 15, 1954   H. W.

CONTENTS

CONTENTS

INTRODUCTION: JAPAN
AND THE UNITED STATES

AMERICA'S POSITION IN REGARD TO JAPAN

By the surrender terms of September, 1945, Japan's armed forces capitulated and the country was occupied by Allied Forces. The Imperial Japanese government continued to function; however, it received its policy directives from the occupation authority embodied in the Supreme Commander for the Allied Powers (SCAP). In theory the occupation government represented the governments of all the Allies, but in practice the powers of the Supreme Commander were such as to make his voice—and hence that of the United States—the deciding factor in occupation policy. When the Treaty of Peace came into force in April, 1952, the occupation came to an end, and Japan regained her sovereignty.

A stipulation of the initial surrender terms deprived Japan of her Army and Navy on the theory that these constituted the last remaining threat to the peace of the Far East. The Japanese, in an earnest affirmation of their peaceful intentions, denied themselves the right to belligerency for all time when they adopted their new Constitution in 1947. It has since become apparent that this gesture was unrealistic, as it failed to leave Japan any means of protecting herself from the growing communist menace in the Far East. In the presence of the resulting power vacuum, the United States has had to undertake the defense of Japan until such time as the Japanese find the will, the resources, and a constitutional means of reassuming their share of the burden. Originally, the maintenance of troops and military installations in Japan was a natural function of the occupation. Thus in June, 1950, it was possible for the United Nations forces fighting in Korea to use bases in Japan. However, Japan's resumption of full sovereignty after the peace treaty necessitated her consent to the continued stationing of American forces on Japanese soil. Such consent was given in a security treaty and a detailed administrative agreement, which came into effect simultaneously with the Treaty of Peace.

SOME PROBLEMS

Public pronouncements from both sides of the Pacific attest to the willingness of both Japan and the United States to stand together politically, militarily, and economically. In the United States, however, these pronouncements have all too often bred either an overconfident belief that the current amity will continue or an apathetic attitude that whatever happens to Japan is of no great concern to Americans. If only to counteract these prevailing moods, a note of caution is in order. Despite the cooperation of the two governments and evidences of friendliness between the two peoples, possible sources of future friction do exist. Some of the more noteworthy of them are indicated below.

1. The rearmament of Japan is regarded in the United States as a necessary and sensible means of reducing the communist

threat. Most Japanese, weary of war and apprehensive that Japan may again become a battlefield, see the rearmament issue in an entirely different light. Many fear a resurgence of Japanese militarism. Still more wishfully think that disarmed neutrality offers them a better chance of survival in another war than active belligerence on either side.

2. Despite a generally good record of behavior by American troops in Japan, their continued presence nine years after the surrender unavoidably causes resentment among Japanese. Specific grievances have been the extraterritorial privileges granted to the American security forces, the increase of prostitution near military installations, a small but well-publicized number of occupation babies of mixed race, and a fear that the national way of life is becoming overly Americanized.

3. The territories which Japan lost as a result of military defeat included the Ryukyu and Bonin Islands, which the Japanese claim by right of long settlement, not military aggression. Irredentist antagonism toward the United States, the present administering authority, is a natural consequence. Return to Japanese control of the northern Ryukyus by the United States in December, 1953, may partially appease this sentiment; however, the strategic importance of Okinawa makes it unlikely that the United States will be willing fully to satisfy Japanese territorial desires, at least in the foreseeable future.

4. Possibly the most immediate danger of friction between America and Japan lies in the conflicting views of the two countries on Japanese trade with Communist China. The disagreement is a clear-cut instance of the possible incompatibilities between Japanese economic demands on the one hand and American military policy on the other. In the long run, it seems

likely that Japan will need mainland goods and markets which are now denied by American embargoes. Since Chinese demands for Japanese products are to a large extent limited to goods that could be used to build up communist military strength, it is extremely unlikely that the United States, under the present circumstances of international politics, will take kindly to renewal of full trade between the two countries. Positions so flatly contradictory as these might eventually lead to a serious rupture in Japanese-American relations.

5. While at the present time trade rivalry between Japan and the United States is not strong, certain Japanese exports to the United States, notably tuna and pottery, have caused concern among American producers and led to pressure on Congress for increased tariffs. Dependent as they are on international trade, the Japanese are extremely sensitive to all such moves which directly affect their livelihood. It appears likely that tariff problems will be an irritant in relations between the two countries for some years to come.

It should not be overlooked that there exist on both sides of the Pacific certain groups that either deliberately seek or unwittingly abet friction between the United States and Japan. Chief of these on the Japanese side are a small but fanatical communist minority, which can be expected to exaggerate and exploit every difference of opinion between Japan and the United States; the opposition parties, which because of the pro-American policies of the present government are frequently forced into the tactical position of making proposals which have an anti-American cast; socialists, who fear that the present rearmament program inspired by the United States can be achieved only at the sacrifice of vital social gains made in recent years; and a considerable number of the intelligentsia, who are inclined to regard American cultural achievements as inferior to those of Europe and Asia.

Despite the fact that organized anti-Japanese sentiment in the United States has disappeared, there still exist in this country certain groups that could bring about a deterioration in the relations between the two nations. These include high-tariff interests, the success of whose efforts might well wreck Japan's already precarious economy, and isolationist groups, whose desire to withdraw from Far Eastern commitments raises Japanese fears that Japan will be abandoned and left to face the Soviet Union and Red China alone.

Nevertheless, it must be granted that most Americans and Japanese appear to be satisfied with the present close alignment of the two countries. If some Americans have doubts about the ability of the Japanese to maintain their new-found political liberties and to avoid a resurgence of militaristic expansionism, they are at least content to adopt a wait-and-see attitude. If certain Japanese groups would prefer to adopt a course of neutralism rather than alignment with the United States, the majority of voters up to the present have been willing to support a government strongly committed to the free world. So long as the Japanese people remain convinced that their present international position offers them the best hope of avoiding war and hunger, two omnipresent fears that far overshadow the fear of communism, Japan can be expected to continue close cooperation with the West. Should they become disillusioned in this regard, their fear of war may breed further neutralism toward the East-West struggle, and their fear of hunger might easily lead them to attempt a solution in totalitarianism, be it of the right or of the left.

READINGS

Reischauer, Edwin O. *The United States and Japan*. Cambridge, Harvard University Press, 1950.

Reischauer, Edwin O., and others. *Japan and America Today*. Stanford, Stanford University Press, 1953.

AN INTRODUCTION
TO JAPAN

Consonants in Japanese have generally the same sound as in English, except that *g* is always hard. Vowels are as in Italian or as in the musical scale: *a* as in *fa*, *i* as in *mi*, *e* as in *re*, *o* as in *do; u* is like *oo* in *boot*. There is an almost even stress on every syllable, a syllable consisting of a consonant-vowel combination. A few syllables end with *n*, for example, the first syllable of *Man'yô-shû*. Vowels marked with a circumflex (Kantô, Kyôto) have approximately twice the time value of unmarked vowels.

Because of generally established usage, certain proper nouns are not marked. For readers who may be interested in knowing the pronunciation, however, these are the names of the islands —Hokkaidô, Honshû, Kyûshû, and Ryûkyû—and of the cities —Tôkyô, Ôsaka, Kôbe, and Kyôto. The *y* in these words is in effect a consonant: the *kyô* of Tôkyô is one syllable, and Kyûshû is pronounced Cue-shoo. Double consonants are both pronounced. In vowel combinations such as *ai* both are pronounced, but rapidly, so that the sound is similar to the pronoun *I* in English.

LAND AND THE PEOPLE

LOCATION, SIZE, AND REGIONS

Japan consists of four main islands and many adjacent smaller ones, a total land area of 142,300 square miles. (Montana, among American states, compares most closely, with 145,878 square miles.) Honshu is the central island and Hokkaido lies due north of it. Shikoku is south of western Honshu across the Inland Sea, and Kyushu completes the group at the southwest extremity. The archipelago spans a range of latitude from roughly 30° to 46° north (approximately New Orleans to Minneapolis or Jacksonville to Montreal). Honshu, with five eighths of the total area and three quarters of the population, is divided for convenience into at least three unofficial regions— northern, central, and western—each of which has its own distinguishing geographical, climatic, and economic characteristics. Northern Honshu extends roughly northward from about the Tokyo Bay area and is commonly referred to as the Tôhoku, or northeast region. Central Honshu extends from the metropolitan areas of Tokyo and Yokohama to those of Osaka and Kobe. The Tokyo Bay cities dominate an area of central Honshu known as the Kantô, which is the governmental and commercial center of the nation. Kyoto, the old capital, and the neighboring industrial and shipping centers of Osaka and Kobe are situated in the other major region of central Honshu, the Kansai. Another great metropolitan area, that of Nagoya, lies near the boundary between Kantô and Kansai. Western Honshu is a narrow peninsula thrust westward from the Kansai district between the Inland Sea and the Japan Sea and is called Chûgoku.

The islands of Japan arch around two sides of the Japan Sea, which separates them from Korea and the Maritime Province of the Soviet Union. Japan, like England, prizes her "splendid isolation" from her continental neighbors, though the isolation in Japan's case is more complete. One cannot, after all, swim the Korea Strait—120 miles—which separates western Honshu from Pusan, Korea. Russia's Far Eastern port of Vladivostok is over four hundred miles across the Japan Sea from northern Japan. In the extreme northeast, postwar occupation by the Soviet Union of islands in the Kurile chain, literally within earshot of northern Hokkaido, brings a traditional enemy closer to Japanese home ground than ever before in Japan's modern history.

Limited by her seashores and by international agreements, Japan's capacity for feeding her people is further restricted by the ruggedness of the terrain. About three fourths of the country is nonarable, that is, too steeply graded for crop cultivation. The population, increasing steadily over the past hundred years, long ago outstripped the available agricultural land and made it impossible for Japan to be even quantitatively self-sufficient in basic necessities. Industry and overseas commerce will always be required to redress the balance. It is sheer necessity that has made Japan a natural maritime nation.

Map of Japan

Japan Sea

Honshû

Hokkaidô

Sapporo

Muroran

Hakodate

Aomori

Tôhoku

Niigata

Sendai

Chûbu

Kansai

Chûgoku

Ôt.

Nikkô

TOKYO

Kyôto

Nagoya

Mt. Fuji

Kôbe

Ôsaka

Yokohama

Tsushima

Okayama

Nara

Kamakura

Shimonoseki

Hiroshima

Kantô

Môji

Beppu

Nagasaki

Kyushu

Shikoku

Pacific Ocean

Japan is an Asian nation by tradition; her cultural roots must be sought in Korea, China, and India. Her economic life still continues to be conditioned by the circumstances of Far Eastern commerce. Yet it is of major importance to Japan's recent history that she has become to an increasing degree a Pacific nation, linked by transoceanic commerce to the community of nations that includes Australia, New Zealand, Chile, Mexico, the United States, and Canada.

CLIMATE

Japan's latitude makes for a temperate climate. Temperatures tend to range higher than in similar latitudes in eastern North America due to the influence of the Japan Current, a tropical stream that flows northeast along Japan's east (Pacific) coast. The same current accounts for the higher average winter temperatures south and east of Japan's central mountain ranges than along the Japan Sea coast.

Rainfall is heavy, ranging from 40 to 100 inches annually. The Pacific coast has strikingly heavier precipitation than the Japan Sea area. Snowfall is frequent and heavy in northern Japan. Seasonal variations are more or less well marked in all parts of the country, particularly in the central and northern portions. All seasons are humid and both summers and winters are, as a consequence, unpleasant. Rainfall is heaviest during a dispiriting season of June and July known as the *bai-u*. Autumn, with bright, crisp weather, is delightful. Winters, except in the far north, rarely approach the miseries associated with that time of year in mid-continental or eastern America. Spring is pleasant, though damp, and is spectacular more for its bursts of blossoms

—plum, cherry, or peach—than for any sudden change from cold to warm weather.

TOPOGRAPHY

Japan's many mountain ranges have a fundamental economic significance. Useful in that they provide timber and make cheap water power available, they are all but useless for habitation or farming. The Japanese islands are of volcanic origin and more than fifty active volcanoes remain, clustered most profusely in Hokkaido, central Honshu, and Kyushu. The highest altitudes, respectively, of these three areas are: Asahi-dake (or Taisetsu-zan), 7,513 feet above sea level; Fuji-san (Mt. Fuji), 12,395 feet; and Yae-shima, 6,348 feet.

Japan is the most actively volcanic region within the world's principal "earthquake belt," which rings the Pacific from New Zealand by way of Alaska to the Strait of Magellan. Seismographs record thousands of disturbances annually, though most of these are too weak to be destructive. Major earthquakes are not infrequent, however, and can be terrible destroyers of life and property. The Kantô earthquake of September 1, 1923, which took upwards of 40,000 lives, was one of the greatest natural disasters in man's recorded history.

There are few extensive plains in Japan, but these are of great economic importance; they support a substantial part of the population and provide much of the food supply. The largest of them is the Kantô plain adjoining Tokyo Bay; others of importance are the Kinki region, including the Kansai cities, and the Chikugo plain of northern Kyushu.

The complex coast line totals 17,150 miles (about twice that of the United States). Harbors are numerous; some of them, including the two principal ones, Yokohama and Kobe, have been dredged to permit access to ocean-going vessels.

POPULATION

The census of 1950 showed a total population for Japan of 83,200,000 (40,791,000 were male and 42,409,000 female—a ratio of 96.2 males per 100 females).

The following table shows national totals and sex distribution for significant years.

Year	National Total	Males per 100 Females
1920	55,391,000	100.5
1930	63,872,000	101.1
1940	72,540,000	100.1
1945 (November)	71,998,000	. . . .
1947	78,101,000	95.4
1950	83,200,000	96.2

The proportion of urban population to the national total rose from 18 percent in 1920 to 37.7 percent in 1940. Wartime evacuation of cities and the destruction of urban housing resulted in a sharp drop in the figure to 28.7 percent in 1945; but the postwar movement to cities has been equally remarkable (due in part to the resettlement of nationals repatriated from Japan's former colonies and occupied territories), and the ratio of urban population to the total now stands at 37.5 percent. Japan has six cities approaching or surpassing 1,000,000 in population and sixty-four exceeding 100,000. Tokyo, the capital, had 5,385,071 in 1950; Osaka had 1,956,136.

Japan's serious population problem may be comprehended

from three facts: the population has increased nearly threefold since the first modern census in 1872; the excess of the birth rate over the death rate is one of the highest on earth; finally, the present population density (226 per square kilometer in 1950) permits virtually no expansion. There has in a sense been a population problem for centuries. Population pressure in the areas first settled accounted for the expansion of the Japanese people from their homelands in northern Kyushu, the Kansai, and Chûgoku districts, first to southern Kyushu and the Kantô and later to northern Honshu and the other islands of the group. Exploitation of marginal land in the centuries after all the main islands were settled afforded more room for population growth. Industrialization in the past century stimulated further growth by increasing the total national wealth, while overseas colonies before the war provided both a convenient source for commercial wealth and *lebensraum* for those Japanese who were enterprising enough to emigrate. Stripped of her colonies and with her industrial and commercial potential impaired by years of war, the nation is confronted with a sobering truth: the population is increasing steadily; the food supply is not.

READINGS

Cressey, George B. *Asia's Lands and Peoples; a Geography of One-Third the Earth and Two-Thirds Its People*. 2nd ed. New York, McGraw-Hill, 1951.

Japan Travel Bureau. *Japanese Tourist Library*. Tokyo. This collection of brochures on the culture of Japan is now in process of revision and expansion. For listing of books available and to be published, consult lists prepared by the Japan Travel Information Office, 10 Rockefeller Plaza, New York 20, N.Y.

Tourist Industry Division, Ministry of Transportation (ed.). *Japan, The Official Guide*. Revised. Tokyo, Japan Travel Bureau, 1952.

FILMS

Japan, Land and People. Coronet Films, Coronet Plaza, Chicago 1, Ill.

Japanese Fishing Village. Young America Films Inc., 18 E. 41st St., New York 17, New York.

Rice Farming in Japan. University of Michigan, Audio-Visual Education Center, 4028 Administration Building, Ann Arbor, Michigan.

So Small My Island. Pan American World Airways, 28–19 Bridge Plaza North, Long Island City, New York.

HISTORY

In Japanese mythology, the nation's history began in 660 B.C., the year in which the first Emperor is said to have subdued the central provinces and ascended the throne. (The date was arrived at much later by calculating backwards in even Chinese calendrical cycles of sixty years; it means very little and in any case is considered at least six centuries too early for the origin of a real Japanese "dynasty.")

Archaeologists have found no traces in Japan of paleolithic settlement, but they agree in the identification of two neolithic cultures, the earlier of which seems to have existed from about the third millennium B.C. The second replaced it in the centuries just before the Christian era. Its artifacts seem to have belonged to a completely different race of people, though both cultures are conjectured to have come to Japan from northern Asia via Korea. Neither race should be called "Japanese." The Ainu stock of present-day northern Japan presumably descends from the earlier race, while the modern Japanese may be descended from a fusion of these two races and others perhaps from southern Asia or the islands of the southwest Pacific.

Archaeological evidence from early in the Christian era indicates a bronze age culture in contact with those of China and

Korea. This evidence is confirmed by Chinese texts from about the same time in which Japan is spoken of as a collection of "kingdoms," inhabited by a people intelligent, warlike, and primitive. These developed a complex tribal society organized around hereditary clans of officials, warriors, and artisans. One such clan in one of the kingdoms came much later to be called "Imperial" (the word and concept were Chinese). The earliest Japanese accounts of their own history are legendary chronicles of the origins of this clan (it was divine and descended from heaven), and of its conquest of all the other Japanese kingdoms and its organization of a centralized state.

Primitive Japanese religion conceived of the supernatural as dwelling in all the objects and forces of nature. Supernatural beings were called *kami* and the religion came to be called *Shintô,* the "Way of the *kami.*" Statecraft in this age was an aspect of religion, for it sought to control the *kami* behind the forces of sun, rain, fire, and earthquake by means of ritual and at the hands of a divine aristocracy and priesthood. The two roles, governmental and priestly, were both hereditary in the same families, so that Japan at the time was a theocratic aristocracy.

THE SINICIZATION OF JAPAN: NARA (710–794) AND HEIAN (794–1185) PERIODS

About 550 A.D., Buddhism entered Japan. After a century or two, a major revolution—religious, social, cultural, and political—had made Japan a permanent part of the civilization of the Chinese Far East, for Buddhism to the Japanese was the bearer of all the attributes of Chinese civilization, then among the

world's most advanced. The Japanese studied Chinese architecture, sculpture, and painting, adapted the Chinese system of
writing for the representation of their own language, founded
schools on the continental pattern, and learned medicine, as-
tronomy (and a fixed calendar), better methods for casting
metals and fashioning tools, and Chinese music. The most complex component of Chinese culture was the organization of
government and society, with the systems of land tenure, rents,
and taxation that went with them. These the Japanese attempted valiantly to copy, and by 700 A.D. many of the forms of
their political and economic life were Chinese imports. The
ancient "divine" nobility did not pretend to shed their divinity,
but they re-enforced their old religious authority with new concepts of loyalty and responsibility adopted from Confucian
China. The emperor now had a double function: he was at once
the chief priest and a secular ruler.

The Japanese failed to reconstruct in their new state some of
the most important institutions of the Chinese system. For one
thing, the Chinese bureaucracy was in theory open to anyone,
noble or commoner, who could qualify in the competitive civil
service examinations. The Japanese bureaucracy was in practice
manned by aristocrats, descendants of the ancient priestly or
military clans whose authority derived from sanctions of the
native religion. In the Heian period (so called after the capital
was moved from Nara to Heian-kyô, now Kyoto) divergence
from purely Chinese culture grew noticeably. Buddhism, which
remained the most important single religion, came more and
more to be a faith for the people. Japanese artisans, having increased their skill at the crafts, developed them into something
peculiarly Japanese (though it must be remembered that they

never lost a fundamental Far Eastern character rooted in
China). A significant development was the shift of political
power to a hereditary regency, or civil dictatorship, of the
powerful Fujiwara family between the ninth and twelfth centuries. Though emperors continued to reign, their Fujiwara
ministers effectively thwarted most of their urges to rule by
taking advantage of the Throne's very divinity. A sacred ruler
needed a mouthpiece to interpret his will to the people. If, as
was frequently the case, the emperor was a minor related
through his mother to the Fujiwara regent, the job of "inter-
preting" was naturally tantamount to sovereign authority.

Meanwhile, in the provinces, land that the seventh- and
eighth-century law codes from China had placed in the hands
of many small landholders tended to become concentrated in a
few large estates. The means by which this was accomplished
was similar to the European feudal practice of commendation
of land to tax-exempt landlords by farmers better able to pay
local rent in exchange for protection than to pay taxes to an
inept central government. These new, enlarged holdings were
tax free owing to their owners' noble or ecclesiastical stations,
and they came to constitute virtually autonomous states. The
landholders came in time to form a new aristocracy, often called
feudal from the dual political and economic nature of their
tenure. They were a military aristocracy as well, fighting inter-
mittently among themselves and engaging in constant warfare
to expand the frontiers of Japanese settlement against the Ainus
of the north. About 1150, two families of provincial nobility
contended for supremacy. A general of the Taira clan first
usurped civil authority previously reserved for Fujiwara ministers. Then after a civil war with the rival Minamoto clan—

the heroic age of later poets and chroniclers—Taira supremacy collapsed, a Minamoto general named Yoritomo took command, and a new age of centralized military dictatorship had commenced.

MILITARY DICTATORSHIP TO 1600: KAMAKURA (1185–1333), MUROMACHI (1333–1568), AND MOMOYAMA (1568–1600) PERIODS

Minamoto Yoritomo established an institution which was to last through numerous vicissitudes from 1192 to 1868. This was the *Bakufu,* or "tent-government," which superseded the civil bureaucracy of the Heian period. Yoritomo reigned under the title *Shôgun,* or General-in-Chief. A man of the field and the provinces, Yoritomo founded his new military capital at Kamakura, far to the east of Kyoto, near the site of modern Tokyo. He was in theory a military officer of the Crown, but for the most part he spared himself the trouble of consulting the Throne on matters of state policy. The *Bakufu* controlled each of the provinces through a constable loyal to Yoritomo. Knights newly confirmed by Yoritomo were the landholders in this system and were largely independent but for the defensive obligations they owed the *Bakufu.* Kamakura law was nothing more than an extension on a national scale of the clan law of the Minamoto family. It did not supplant the civil government but supplemented it; emperor, ministers, and civil bureaucrats—even the hereditary Fujiwara regency—continued to exist in Kyoto, but there the titles were increasingly empty and those who held them increasingly powerless.

The centralized military dictatorship of Kamakura was tested in 1274 and 1281 by Japan's only historic invasions from abroad, by the Mongols under Kublai Khan. Though the Khans had built an empire stretching from China across central Asia to Lithuania, they failed to conquer Japan, due to a fortunate conjunction of Japanese prowess at arms and a typhoon in the Strait of Tsushima (the now legendary *kamikaze,* or "divine wind"), which destroyed the second invading fleet. Though the victory assured Japan her independence, it foretold the collapse of the national unity that the *Bakufu* had purchased at so great a cost of arms. The cost of outfitting the defensive forces ruined the *Bakufu* financially but, more important, it encouraged independence in the outside lords, who were then in a position to contend for military supremacy.

A new dynasty of shoguns, the Ashikaga, provided fifteen rulers from 1338 until late in the sixteenth century, but most of them failed in the attempt to give the nation unified, secure government. Dissident military families fought the shogun and one another continuously for control of territory. Rarely were more than the central provinces under the shogun's control. For many years in the fourteenth century an Ashikaga shogun held court in Kyoto with an emperor of his own sponsorship, while a rival emperor commanded the allegiance of other military families from a fortress-court fifty miles to the south at Yoshino. Warfare was intermittent during the entire period and after about 1470 was continuous throughout the country.

Trade relations with the Continent, which had languished in the long period after the first fruitful contacts, flourished again in the fifteenth and sixteenth centuries. Encouraged by the central government, other Japanese *daimyô,* or feudal lords, traded with China and southeast Asia (their men sometimes in the role of pirates); they established a network of maritime influence of much importance to the history of oriental commerce.

In 1542 Portuguese traders landed in Kyushu and were followed in the next few years by Portuguese and Spanish missionaries who set out to convert Japan to Christianity. By the early seventeenth century, there were about 300,000 Japanese Christians; yet, for the most part, the effect of early Western contacts on Japan was not religious but military and political. When it appeared that Western nations had political designs on Eastern peoples, the Japanese nobles grew cautious in their attitude toward them. They gladly accepted Western improvements in arms and defense—musket design and castle architecture, for example—and were willing in some instances to Christianize their subjects in the hope of foreign military alliance against domestic enemies. They came to mistrust, then to reject, Christianity when they realized it might be a predecessor to subversion and conquest.

These unsettled times made military prowess more important than ancestry as a measure of social prestige. Scions of old aristocracy lost lands and status, whereas brave upstarts found themselves masters of provinces. The new maritime commerce and the need for permanent, expensive fortifications gave birth to cities, where a new social class of merchants dealing in coin and credit was to displace the simple agricultural and barter economy of older times.

Between 1565 and 1600, three military men led the reunification of Japan. The first of them, the minor territorial lord Oda Nobunaga, conquered many of the provinces of central Japan and broke the power, then formidable, of the large Buddhist monasteries. On his murder in 1582, his forces and lands fell to his foremost general, a remarkable soldier of peasant stock named Hideyoshi, who conquered or allied with the states of western Japan. From his new castle at Osaka he reigned as Prime Minister and Civil Dictator, titles which none but aristocrats had ever assumed. The nation unified and pacified, Hideyoshi sought a means of keeping his country's vast soldiery from thoughts of rebellion. An abortive invasion of Korea (with the conquest of China its eventual aim) was the result— Japan's only overseas war between the seventh and nineteenth centuries. Hideyoshi died in 1598 while Japanese troops were still in Korea. His greatest general and successor was Tokugawa Ieyasu, who, unlike Hideyoshi, was of aristocratic stock but, like him, was a self-made man.

THE TOKUGAWA PERIOD (1600–1868)

Tokugawa Ieyasu's problem in 1598 was to reinforce Hideyoshi's precarious military union with an efficient administrative system and the strength of law. In 1603 he had himself named hereditary Shogun. Political stability in monarchical Japan demanded a dynasty, and Ieyasu founded the line which was to govern until 1868.

Europeans in Japan labored under increasing difficulties under Hideyoshi and Ieyasu. Fear of Catholic conquest prompted Hideyoshi in 1587 to ban all missionaries from Japan. Proscription of Christianity after 1600 eventuated in bloody persecution of the European missionaries and their Japanese converts; and finally in 1637 a full-scale rebellion at the western Kyushu outpost of Shimabara, in which 37,000 die-hard Japanese Christians were killed by the Shogun's armies, virtually did away with Christianity as an organized religion in Japan. In 1624 the third Tokugawa Shogun had expelled all Spaniards from Japan. By 1640 decrees were in force which excluded all Europeans from Japan as a whole, forbade Japanese from traveling abroad, and limited merchant vessels to a certain tonnage insufficient for overseas navigation. One small window was left open to foreign trade—and foreign cultural influence. Chinese and Dutch merchants were allowed to trade with official Japanese middlemen at Nagasaki. With a few exceptions the Dutch here provided Japan's only lawful contact with Europe for over two hundred years.

The peace and security that the Tokugawa shoguns gave Japan for two and a half centuries depended on a complex balance of forces—political, military, and economic. The shogun held certain lands outright (including his military capital at Edo, now Tokyo, and the commercial cities of Osaka and Nagasaki) or entrusted them to relatives or direct hereditary vassals (*fudai daimyô*). The "outside lords" (*tozama daimyô*), who submitted to Tokugawa rule at sword's point after 1600, were rendered harmless by isolating them in areas outside the central provinces and by severe restrictions on alliances among them. The system was in effect a close alliance of military states independent of the *Bakufu* in many of their internal affairs but strictly controlled by it in their relations with one another. Another source of national unity was the vague influence of the powerless emperor and his effete court at Kyoto, under the constant surveillance of a shogunal deputy.

All daimyo were allotted fiefs of land assessed in terms of annual rice yield. The daimyo in turn paid their samurai (the

military, professional, and official class) fixed incomes reckoned
in terms of rice. Taxation was exacted from the peasantry in
food crops and exchange was to a large extent in the form of
barter. Yet Tokugawa economy was increasingly one of agri-
culture-plus-commerce, and the commercial wealth of the growing cities steadily tended to upset the purely agricultural economy that existed in theory. Economically the history of Japan
in the Tokugawa period is the story of the rising merchant
class's acquisition of more and more of the wealth of the govern-
ing classes, daimyo and samurai. With wealth came a distinctive
city culture fostered by the merchant classes. Wealthy commoners began to buy or marry their way into the samurai class
and in the process produced a new aristocracy partly of inheritance from the feudal nobility and partly of wealth.

The lot of the peasantry in the Tokugawa period was never
easy; in years of poor crops or times of disaster from fires, floods,
or earthquakes, it was bleak indeed. Agrarian revolts were
numerous, but they were minor uprisings, many bloodless, to
redress specific grievances in local areas rather than against the
Bakufu itself. The authorities had little to fear from popular
revolution. As the economy expanded in these years of peace
through the seventeenth and eighteenth centuries, the standard
of living increased somewhat, though possibilities in that direction were naturally limited by the frozen economy of a nation
locked against foreign trade.

Two revolutionary developments of the nineteenth century
transformed Japan into a modern nation. By the first of them
she reopened her harbors to foreign ships, encouraged her
citizens to learn from the West, and began her amazingly
rapid rise to the status of a world power. By the second, she

abolished feudalism and the system of dual government, shogunal and imperial, which had lasted for nearly seven hundred
years. Forces inside and outside Japan effected these changes.
Dissatisfaction against the shogun's authority was growing in
many classes of society in the early part of the century and a
few rebels looked forward to the restitution of the ancient
Imperial House to supremacy as an instrument of state, not
merely an ornamental symbol of national continuity. Certain
tozama daimyô, notably the most powerful of those in western
Japan, in Chôshû (western Honshu), and Satsuma (southern
Kyushu), had wealth and military power rivaling that of the
Bakufu and in coalition might hope to overthrow it. Scholars
chafed under the seclusion edicts, which had been relaxed somewhat in 1720 to permit the introduction of European scientific
and medical information to Japan, a step which only whetted
the appetite for still more knowledge from the West.

After 1825 a series of attempts by Western powers to force an
end to seclusion had as objectives guarantees of the care and
safe return of shipwrecked sailors, provision of fueling ports,
and the exploitation of a new field for commercial and missionary activity. It culminated in the successful Perry mission
of 1853. Commodore Matthew Calbraith Perry obtained on
behalf of the United States a shipwreck convention and also
exacted from the *Bakufu* a promise to open diplomatic negotiations in the near future. America's first envoy, Townsend
Harris, arrived in 1856 and two years later negotiated the treaty
that formally opened Japan to relations with the West. Similar
treaties with European powers followed shortly thereafter.

Reaction by the *Bakufu's* conservative enemies was instan-
taneous. Outrages against the hated foreigners increased. When

an Englishman was murdered outside the new foreign port of Yokohama by samurai in the entourage of the daimyo of Satsuma, the British retaliated by bombarding the fief's capital of Kagoshima. The foreign supremacy of arms thus evidenced did not noticeably mollify Satsuma's hostility to trade (which one must remember was to be on terms imposed by the foreigners), but it did waken Japan to the necessity of strengthening national defenses if foreign demands were to be resisted. The battle cry of the dissidents at this time was, "Revere the Emperor; expel the barbarians." The prestige of the Imperial Court was called to aid in the crisis by the Shogun himself, who feared to assume sole responsibility for the revolutionary decisions he felt he must make. In 1865 the Throne acceded to the Shogun's request that additional ports be opened to foreign trade, but the Shogun had lost much prestige merely by making the request. At last a Shogun friendly to the Imperial cause took office and in 1867 abdicated to a new civilian government responsible to the Emperor alone.

THE MEIJI PERIOD

The Revolution of 1868 was a "restoration" to power of the Imperial dynasty, then embodied in a fifteen-year-old boy whose reign name (1868–1912) was Meiji. The Charter Oath pronounced by the Emperor at his removal to the Shogun's capital, then renamed Tokyo, was a hopefully liberal document calling for freedom of occupation, abolition of worn-out laws and customs, and deliberative assemblies representing "public opinion." The era was one of modernization of most phases of the national life. The government accomplished industrialization and achieved military preparedness with great speed and efficiency, but this entailed an inevitable sacrifice of the liberalism voiced in the Charter Oath. The Restoration leaders were for the most part young samurai of the great western fiefs plus a few bluebloods of the Kyoto nobility and former functionaries of the *Bakufu*. These men became a self-perpetuating oligarchy far more influential in the Meiji government than the Emperor himself. Some of the more important of them are mentioned here:

Iwakura Tomomi, Kido Kôin, Ôkubo Toshimichi, and Itô Hirobumi, in a series of policy decisions of the early seventies, set the national course for internal reforms, industrialization, and the establishment of a strong, centralized state.

Saigô Takamori, a model of samurai loyalty and courage, opposed them in favor of an aggressive foreign and military policy.

Yamagata Aritomo, founder of the modern Japanese Army, was in some ways most powerful of all the oligarchs. He introduced conscription, patterned the Army on the German model (after German victory in the Franco-Prussian War), and worked for fifty years to make Japan a world power and the Army a formidable instrument of state within it.

Whatever their differences, these men were united in their conviction that they alone had the necessary experience and responsibility to direct the affairs of state. All of them but the court noble Iwakura were samurai of Chôshû or Satsuma and made of those clans a virtual aristocracy within an aristocracy.

Itagaki Taisuke of Tosa and Ôkuma Shigenobu of Hizen were the most eminent of this clique's opponents through the 1870's and 1880's. Their weapons were two European institutions that might in time break the power of the Council of State: parliamentary government and the political party. For whatever personal motives, these two men were foremost of the founders of Japanese liberalism.

The government abolished feudalism between 1869 and 1876. Daimyo surrendered their fiefs to the Throne, local administrative units were established subordinate to the central government, and the samurai were reduced from being hereditary arms-bearers and pensioners to the status of commoners. Resentment among the more conservative samurai, particularly those of Satsuma who were attracted by the forceful personality of Saigô Takamori, culminated in a rebellion against the government forces. The victory of Yamagata's conscripts over Saigô's aristocrats in 1877 destroyed more of the past perhaps than had the Restoration itself.

Some of the oligarchs, Ôkubo and Itô among them, realized that parliamentary government was a feature of the strongest Western powers and thought it an eventual goal for Japan if she were to become fully modernized. On the other hand, they resented any diminution of personal power and resisted every attempt to broaden the base of government. Repression of parliamentary sentiment flared up as late as 1878, when Ôkubo was assassinated for his conservatism. Itagaki and Ôkuma, the former safely outside the government and the latter about to leave it, forced the hand of the clan oligarchs by exposing their graft and corruption and obtained the promise of a National Diet to be convened nine years later (1890). With elections in the offing, Japan's first political parties made their appearance. Itagaki's Liberal Party (*Jiyû-tô*) catered to the farmer and small-propertied classes, whereas Ôkuma's Progressives (*Kaishin-tô*) favored the economic and intellectual upper classes. The government "ins" countered ineffectually with a party of their own, the Imperial Government Party (*Teisei-tô*), Imperial rule to these men meaning their own continuance in power. Itô Hirobumi made a trip to Europe to study existing parliaments. Theoretically free to choose between an oligarchic German or liberal English model, Itô decided on the German as better suited to Japan's needs and to preserving imperial rule. Hence the Prussian-style cabinet which replaced the Council of State in 1885 was a powerful and self-perpetuating executive body of clan bureaucrats. A constitution, promulgated in 1889, appeased further liberal demands, but in effect it merely confirmed continued rule of the oligarchy. The National Diet of 1890 was elected by a limited body of voters; its powers were severely restricted by executive prerogatives of the cabinet.

Though the adoption of Western parliamentarianism failed to produce truly liberal political institutions, Japanese economic modernization on Western lines was phenomenally successful. Enterprising merchants and financiers started that process of concentration of capital which produced the "financial clique" (*zaibatsu*) in later years. Zaibatsu firms organized an electric power system and built the great textile and coal industries. The demand for native-controlled shipping produced the O.S.K. (Osaka Shôsen Kaisha) and N.Y.K. (Nippon Yûsen Kaisha) lines, both in operation by 1885. The government educated the public in the operations of finance capital from 1870 on and encouraged the establishment of banks, insurance companies, and commodities exchanges. In 1882 Finance Minister Matsukata Masayoshi led the foundation of a central banking agency, The Bank of Japan (modeled after the Bank of Belgium), with powers to issue convertible bank notes, to regulate the national currency and foreign exchange of specie and bullion, and to furnish capital to banks and businesses.

As military preparedness was the principal aim of industrialization, munitions plants, heavy industries, and communications facilities were the first to be modernized. Many goods for domestic consumption continued to be produced under the ancient cottage industry system, though within a few decades the factory system introduced for the sake of producing arms was turning out civilian goods as well.

The Department of Education, organized in 1871, concentrated on a program of elementary education to eradicate illiteracy and train a loyal populace in the duties of citizenship. Tokyo University (1877) was the first of the national schools that were to train most of Japan's succeeding civil servants and set the standards for the education of future generations of business and professional leaders. A westernized press served the government's purposes in keeping the public aware of its new responsibilities, but it also offered liberals and dissenters some freedom of expression on all sorts of matters. The proscription of Christianity had been removed in 1872, and the missionary movement, Catholic and Protestant, proceeded apace from that time. Interest in Western religion and philosophy typified the westernizing spirit of the new age.

In the social sphere, the government abolished the samurai and *eta* classes, the latter having been limited for centuries to menial or humiliating occupations and an outcast social status. Women's rights lagged behind other social reforms, but schools for women were established in the seventies and eighties, and women gained legal rights to head households and initiate divorce actions.

Japanese diplomacy between 1870 and the early nineties was aimed at gaining the diplomatic equality with foreign nations that extraterritoriality and most-favored-nation clauses of the early Western treaties specifically denied her. The government set up a Foreign Ministry in 1869 and sent emissaries abroad in 1872 to urge treaty revision by the powers, but decided not to press the matter while Japan was militarily defenseless. The treaty by which Russia recognized the Japanese right to the Kuriles (1875) and China's *de facto* recognition of Japanese sovereignty in the Ryukyus (1884) were diplomatic triumphs that started Japan on her way to wide-scale territorial expansion. Of greater importance were the negotiations over Japan's diplomatic rights in Korea. The Chinese Empire considered Korea a tributary state, whereas Japan claimed she was independent. Japan gained full diplomatic and postal rights in Korea in 1880, but a civil dispute in that country brought China and Japan into another disagreement on the issue of Korean independence. The settlement that Itô Hirobumi obtained from the Chinese Minister Li Hung-Chang (Li–Ito Convention, 1885) provided that neither country could dispatch troops to Korea without previously notifying the other. The real issue in the case was which of the countries was to dominate Korea. The Convention postponed a decision, allowing Japan to concentrate on treaty revision. Great Britain announced the intention of giving up her extraterritorial rights whenever Japan should reform her judicial system to conform to Western standards. Further negotiations led to treaties (1894–99) granting full judicial sovereignty, while full tariff autonomy came with the U.S.–Japanese Treaty of Commerce and Navigation of 1911.

The Sino-Japanese War of 1894–95 confirmed Japan's position as a Far Eastern power, and the Russo-Japanese War of 1904–5 made her a world power. Both conflicts concerned foreign influence in Korea and Manchuria. The former gained for Japan Western admiration of her strength; it gave her Formosa and the Pescadores; it won for her several commercial advantages in China. The peace treaty originally granted Japan the Liaotung Peninsula (on the Manchurian coast), but the so-called Triple Intervention of Russia, France, and Germany forced her to give up this prize. (Popular rancor in Japan at this move was of lasting effect in the modification of future foreign policy.) China's antiforeign Boxer Uprising of 1900 gave Japan an opportunity to confirm her status as a power when the others requested that she send a large share of the troops to quell it, but it worked also to Russia's advantage by deflecting the attention of the powers from her simultaneous occupation of Manchuria. The Anglo-Japanese Alliance of 1902 was in recognition of the threat which European, particularly Russian, designs on Chinese and Korean territorial integrity held for the peace of the Far East. Backed by English friendship, Japan could undertake a war with Russia without fear of intervention by a third power. Japanese victory over Russia (1905) assured her "paramount political, military, and economic interests" in Korea, secured in Manchuria the special railroad and commercial rights which had been Russia's, and gave her southern Sakhalin. The Japanese public were disappointed that the Treaty of Portsmouth did not grant still more concessions, but Japan's world position was assured by it.

As a result, Japanese-American relations became of greater moment. Two principal points were at issue: (1) commercial rivalry in China and (2) Japanese immigration to America. Proximity plus the 1905 concessions gave Japan advantages in the China trade. Korea was virtually a Japanese colony after 1907, actually so after 1910. The Root-Takahira agreement of 1908 alleviated tension by guaranteeing mutual respect of the other nation's rights and possessions in the Far East. Meanwhile, feelings against Japanese immigrants in America's western states mounted. Cheap oriental labor was thought to be a threat to the standard of living of American laborers. The Hearst papers and other elements of the California press aggravated the situation, demanding exclusion of Orientals. There was talk of war over the issue, but in 1908 the Japanese themselves relieved the tension by the so-called Gentlemen's Agreement, whereby Japan refused passports to laborers and their families wishing to emigrate to the United States, in return for which the American government was not to affront the national pride by prohibiting Japanese immigration altogether. The American Immigration Law of 1924 was a breach of the Gentlemen's Agreement and created much ill will toward America in Japan.

Japan joined the Allied side in the First World War in August, 1914. The Navy occupied Kiaochow and Tsingtao, the German concession on the China coast, and Germany's Pacific possessions and, by the end of the war, was policing the Indian

Ocean from Australia to South Africa. Japan took advantage of the war to issue demands to China (the Twenty-one Demands) aimed at establishing for Japan a dominant economic and political position on the Continent. Japanese aims at the Versailles Conference were limited primarily to confirmation of her possession of the former German concession in China and cession of Germany's Pacific possessions north of the equator (the Carolines, Marianas, and Marshalls). Both were granted. The war years had been a time of unprecedented prosperity for Japanese business, and the nation emerged as one of the Big Five world powers. Early in 1918, before the end of the war, Japan joined the United States and other Allies in an expedition to Siberia with the aim of putting down the Bolsheviks. American troops withdrew in 1920, but the Japanese remained until 1922, obviously with the objective of capitalizing on the Russian crisis to strengthen Japan's own continental position. By the Treaty of Versailles, Japan had a permanent seat on the Council of the League of Nations. Chinese opposition to Japan's leasehold in Shantung eventually led to relinquishment of the concessions to Chinese sovereignty, though Japan retained a lien on the railways and a Japanese traffic manager.

In an attempt to control economic development of China through an international body and hence forestall further spheres of influence or territorial concessions to individual nations, the United States proposed at the Versailles Conference the establishment of a financial consortium, or international loan-making body. Japan at first refused to participate in it but agreed later when assurances were given that her privileges in Manchuria would not be threatened.

INTERNAL DEVELOPMENTS (1890–1920)

Political history entered a new phase after the convening of the first Diet in 1890. The clan oligarchs continued to dominate the cabinet and further strengthened their position through two extraparliamentary bodies of a conservative nature. The first of these, the *genrô*, or elder statesmen, consisted of past servants of the Imperial cause who came with advancing age to enjoy the special trust of the Emperor and government. The second body, the Privy Council, came into being in 1888 to approve the new Constitution before its promulgation. It had powers of review and veto of legislation as well as advisory functions. The political parties continued to work for strengthening of representative government.

For a decade or so, advocates of party government vied for control with the supporters of oligarchic control. For the first few years, elder statesmen firmly entrenched in the oligarchic cabinet succeeded one another as prime minister—Yamagata, Matsukata, Itô, Matsukata, Itô. Then for a few months in 1898 the newly formed Constitutional Party (*Kensei-tô*) formed a cabinet under the pioneers of liberalism, Itagaki and Ôkuma. The *Kensei-tô*, like succeeding parties, was hardly more than a coalition of individuals dissatisfied with oligarchic rule, and the cabinet it formed collapsed soon after from internal dissensions. Its successor was another government of clan bureaucrats under Yamagata. The Imperial Ordinance of 1900, which this cabinet promulgated, was in later years to do more perhaps than any other single measure to impede the progress of popular or representative government in Japan. The Ordinance remained in effect until after the Second World War and provided that only top-ranking officers of the armed services might hold the posts of War and Navy ministers. Since the services themselves might withdraw their ministers or refuse to recommend new ones, the provision gave them an absolute veto power over the civilian government. An upsurge of chauvinism at the time of the Russo-Japanese War further handicapped truly liberal government. A variety of factions formed succeeding cabinets until the post-First World War governments formed on the basis of Diet composition once more gave promise of party government responsive to the will of the electorate.

The socialist movement in Japan up to the First World War was almost completely dissociated from the constitutional or parliamentary struggle here outlined. Though Itagaki's Liberal Party of the early eighties had social reform aims, the foundations of Japanese radicalism were in the Oriental Socialist Party founded in 1882 and in various labor associations of the 1890's. A political party of 1901 dominated by railway workers was suppressed by the government, while the pacifist leanings of labor groups during the Russo-Japanese War further roused the government against the labor movement as a whole. In 1910 a plot by the radical Socialist, Kôtoku Denjirô, to assassinate the Emperor resulted in violent suppression of all labor organizations, most of which were incomparably more moderate than Kôtoku's anarchists. The incident led to almost complete extirpation of the socialist movement in Japan for more than a decade. Fear of radicalism continued to be a force in Japanese politics and was used by conservatives to thwart many a move toward democracy in the twenties and thirties.

EXPANSION AFTER THE FIRST WORLD WAR

For a few years after the First World War it appeared that militarism and the repression of liberalism were on the way out. The Hara Cabinet of 1918 was the first to be headed by a commoner. Party pluralities in the House of Representatives determined the composition of the cabinet. Internationally, Japan appeared willing to cooperate with the League of Nations and abandon her policy of aggression toward Asia. At the Washington Conference of 1922 she agreed to withdraw from the Anglo-Japanese Alliance, vacate Shantung and Siberia, and reduce naval armaments. In the same year, however, conservatives on the Emperor's advisory councils took direct action to reverse this trend by appointing the first of a series of military men to form cabinets. The American Immigration Act of 1924 embittered the nation and confirmed the existing contempt of its leaders for the sanctity of international agreements. The depletion of Japanese credit due to a temporary collapse in the silk market and overvaluation of the yen contributed to general economic instability, already of serious proportions when the world-wide crash of 1929 struck. The Premier at the time, Hamaguchi Yûkô, by advocating Japanese participation in the London Naval Treaty of 1930, aroused the hatred of the militarists. In September, 1931, a "Manchurian clique" in the Army proceeded independently of the civilian government to instigate the first of a series of "incidents" designed ostensibly to protect Japanese railway interests in Manchuria, but actually aimed at making Manchuria a colony under the sole control of the Army. Manchuria, which had never been under the control of the central government of the Chinese Nationalists, was declared the independent country of Manchoukuo (1932) but was actually a Japanese possession in which the Army tested its plans for a war-directed, controlled economy. Huge government-financed businesses and industries aroused the envy of the Japanese zaibatsu, many of whose members were thereby persuaded to accept managerial positions in the continental development companies.

Assassination of government leaders had been an effective way for dissatisfied elements to make their objections known since before the Restoration. After the murder of Prime Minister Inukai in 1932, this threat hung over any official who opposed the designs of the militarists. Too often the government failed to punish assassins, most of whom were visibly sincere in the "patriotic" motives for their acts. A full-scale coup d'état by young Army extremists in February, 1936, followed a defeat for the ultranationalists at the polls. Three senior ministers among the moderates were killed and the rest of the government, whch included some moderates, was terrorized into submission to the demands of the extremists.

Meanwhile, the Army's continental policy had become more and more aggressive. Japan withdrew from the League of Nations in 1932 when the latter threatened sanctions for the Manchurian Incident. The North Chinese province of Jehol was annexed to Manchoukuo in 1933. In 1935 the "Autonomous" Council of East Hopei brought more North Chinese territory under Japanese military control. A clash between Japanese and Chinese troops at Marco Polo Bridge near Peking in July, 1937, finally launched open war between Japan and the Nationalist government of Chiang Kai-shek. Local Japanese military authorities in China commenced all-out aerial and ground attacks, and the Tokyo government was forced to back them by dispatching troops. Immediate protests by the United States and the League of Nations against this aggression were useless. Japanese troops soon occupied the China coast south to the Yangtze River. The unprovoked attack (December, 1937) on the U.S. gunboat *Panay* in the river above Nanking created serious international tension, threatening war between the two countries, until expressions of regret by the Japanese government and public restored calm. The National Mobilization Law of 1938 and establishment of a puppet government in occupied China brought the nation several steps closer to domination by its expansionist and repressive militarists.

By diverting British and French attention from the Far East, the outbreak of the Second World War gave Japan further opportunities for aggression. Late in 1940, Japan was granted military privileges in Indo-China by the Vichy government. The three-power pact of that time with Germany and Italy gave Japan Axis blessing for any acts she might undertake to complete the conquest of the entire Far East. An economic and political empire centered in Tokyo and embracing all of East Asia (the Greater East Asia Co-Prosperity Sphere) became the dream of Japanese leaders. The aim could be accomplished short of war only if the Axis partnership were maintained and at the same time the United States and the Soviet Union remained neutral. Foreign Minister Matsuoka Yôsuke endeavored through 1941 to appease all sides and to reach an agreement with the Chinese Nationalists, but he made countenance of further aggression a requisite to amity and was hence unsuccessful in appeasing the Western democracies. General Tôjô Hideki became Premier in October of that year and totalitarian military dictatorship was in control. Eight weeks later the attacks on Pearl Harbor and Manila proclaimed the failure of diplomacy as Japan turned the United States from unfriendly neutral to active belligerent in the Second World War.

Japanese leaders relied on American lack of preparedness and the unwillingness of the American people to make necessary sacrifices to assure victory. If the expected German victory in Europe had occurred, Japan might have been able to negotiate a peace with America from a position of great strength in Asia. Admiral Yamamoto's oft-misquoted remark that Japan—to win —would have to dictate peace terms in the White House was an expression of caution from a moderate Navy man chary of Japan's ability to achieve more than partial victory over the United States. When eventual defeat should have been apparent to the government, extremists in the Army still held out for a miracle that never materialized. The war dragged on two or more years after the tide turned against Japan. Atomic bombing of Hiroshima and Nagasaki in August, 1945, was for the purpose not of assuring victory for the Allies, which was certain anyway, but of avoiding the costly invasion of the Japanese islands which the Japanese Army seemed determined to let happen. Russia entered the war the same week and forced troops in Manchuria to capitulate. A cabinet decision, aided by direct intervention of the Emperor, brought hostilities to an end on August 14, 1945.

Surrender terms were formulated by heads of state of the United States, England, and China at Potsdam in July, 1945, and called for surrender of troops and arms, demobilization, and submission to Allied occupation (the United States to be the chief occupying power for the Allies). General Douglas

MacArthur, who had been wartime Commander of Allied Forces in the Southwest Pacific, was named Supreme Commander for the Allied Powers (SCAP). The extent of Japan's defeat may be judged by the statistics: nearly 1,500,000 troops and civilians killed; 30 percent of the urban population homeless; 40 percent of the urban area leveled; industry reduced to 33 percent of its 1936–37 productive capacity. Clearly, reconstruction and rehabilitation were the first problems to be faced. Punishment of war criminals; removal of militarists and their accomplices from positions of responsibility in government, business, and professions; and tutelage of the nation in the mechanics of democratic self-government were stated to be the basic aims of the occupation.

The first phase of the occupation lasted until about 1948, when the initial aims seemed on their way to accomplishment. An elaborate occupation government consisting of sections for the administration of political, economic, and educational policies took its orders from the Supreme Commander and relayed them to the Japanese government. A new Constitution set the pattern for a constitutional monarchy with parliamentary control similar to that in Britain and outlawed war as an instrument of national policy. A land reform program redistributed land in the hands of absentee owners to the farmers who worked it. Military government teams in the prefectures supervised the reorganization of local governments, which were to have greater independence than before. Some capital equipment in the possession of the government was distributed as reparation to Asiatic victims of Japanese aggression. Over four thousand war criminals were punished and thousands more of the nation's former leaders were barred from public office. The educational system was thoroughly reformed, giving greater autonomy to local school boards and outlawing the teaching of militant nationalism. These policies were for the most part conceived and implemented by American authorities, though the British Commonwealth provided occupying troops for some areas and all the wartime Allies nominally supervised the occupation through the Far Eastern Commission of eleven members (later thirteen) in Washington and the Allied Council of four members in Tokyo.

The first postwar elections, in April, 1946, gave the two major conservative parties, the Liberals and the Progressives, a plurality in the House of Representatives and made the Liberal leader, Yoshida Shigeru, Prime Minister. The Communist Party, newly permitted to run candidates, did more poorly than expected, with only 3.8 percent of the popular vote for the House. Elections in April, 1947, under the new laws showed an increase of Socialist strength and gave the premiership to the Socialist leader, Katayama Tetsu. A profusion of political parties made, and still makes, majority government improbable; this government was a coalition including the moderate Democrats and members of the People's Cooperative Party. Internal cabinet shifts made the Democrat Ashida Hitoshi Prime Minister, but the withdrawal of the Socialists and charges of corruption in the government forced general elections in January, 1949. Succeeding cabinets under Yoshida Shigeru have been somewhat more conservative.

Early in the occupation international events began to force American aims in Japan into a radically different direction from that envisaged during the war. Demobilization and demilitarization had been rapid, and democratization, so far as could be determined at the time, had been accomplished to an amazing degree. From 1947 on the American government attempted to bring the occupation to a close through a peace treaty but encountered opposition from the Soviet Union, which had as great a stake in the failure of the Allied reforms as the United States had in their success. Speedy economic rehabilitation for Japan became the major American objective, whereas ironically Japan's defenselessness seemed only to work to the advantage of the Communists. Communist strength at the polls had never been a serious threat, but the hard-core Communist minority in Japan could be counted on to capitalize on the dissatisfactions a long occupation would inevitably entail. After the outbreak of the Korean War in June, 1950, the necessity of launching the United Nations offensive from Japanese soil made Japan's non-sovereign status an increasing embarrassment. In 1951 it was decided to forego the advantages of a joint peace by all the Second World War belligerents, and in September of that year forty-eight nations signed a peace treaty with Japan, Russia abstaining. A security pact with the United States signed at the same time assured Japan of at least temporary defenses without causing her to abandon her constitutional position against the maintenance of armed forces. A national police reserve of 75,000 men had been created in 1950 to relieve some of America's defense burden, but it was obvious after the peace treaty that some means would have to be worked out whereby Japan could assume more of the responsibility for her own defense without falling into the old pitfalls of militarism and aggressive nationalism.

READINGS

Reischauer, Edwin O. *Japan; Past and Present*. 2nd ed., revised and enlarged. New York, Alfred A. Knopf, 1953.

Sansom, George Bailey. *Japan; a Short Cultural History*. Rev. ed. New York, Appleton-Century, 1944.

———— *The Western World and Japan; a Study in the Interaction of European and Asiatic Cultures*. New York, Alfred A. Knopf, 1950.

Yanaga, Chitoshi. *Japan since Perry*. New York, McGraw-Hill, 1949.

GOVERNMENT

The present form of government in Japan dates only from the Constitution of 1947, but many of its features can be traced to much earlier times. Japan's progress toward constitutional democracy can best be understood against the background of the institutions and habits she had inherited from before the war.

GENERAL FEATURES

Prewar Japan was in theory an absolute monarchy. The emperor might, if he chose, declare all the existing laws null and void or declare war or replace all the government officials and functionaries with others more to his liking. The Constitution of 1889 was his "gift" to the people. It outlined the forms under which the actual government operated, but it in no way diminished the supreme authority outside the law which the emperor held by virtue of his "divine" descent. In practice, of course, no emperor ever held such unreserved power. The very sanctity of the position made it unfitting for the sovereign to trouble himself with affairs of practical politics. The elaborate machinery of government consisted of fully competent ministers and bureaucrats whose theoretical role was either to "advise" the emperor or to carry out his commands.

With the single reservation that the emperor *could if he wished* rule with unbridled authority, the government need not have been despotic in practice. Throughout the Meiji and Taishô periods (1868–1926) there was much agitation for parliamentary rule in which the cabinet should be directly responsible to the will of the electorate. Actually, such a state of affairs never came about, primarily because Japan's educated leadership thought in terms of oligarchy and resisted attempts to place government in the hands of the inexperienced masses.

The actual wielders of power varied from time to time in the seventy years before the outbreak of the Second World War. The Meiji Restoration had been led by a few young samurai of the great semi-independent feudal clans of western Japan. These men continued to lead the government in Meiji times. The Council of State until 1885, then all succeeding cabinets from that date until after the First World War, were dominated by members of this clan oligarchy or by their protégés. After 1900 the oligarchy began to be infiltrated increasingly by members of the military caste, for these men, whatever their origins, owed their positions to military organizers within the clan oligarchy such as Field Marshal Yamagata of Chôshû or Admiral Yamamoto of Satsuma. Even the more or less liberal opposition to the Chôshû-Satsuma oligarchy, men like Itagaki Taisuke and Ôkuma Shigenobu, were ex-samurai of other powerful western clans. After 1918 there was a tendency for cabinets to represent majority parties within the Diet, though these governments were powerless to prevent the independent action of extraparliamentary groups such as the Army. Military domination of the civilian government increased after the Manchurian Incident of 1931, giving rise to a new oligarchy of rightist extremists in the Army and Navy and their supporters among the business or bureaucrat classes.

The Imperial Diet had two houses, the House of Peers and the House of Representatives. The former consisted of members of the nobility, men of distinguished service to the state, and high taxpayers. Membership was by Imperial appointment or election by classes represented, and the body was as a consequence very conservative. The House of Representatives represented geographical districts. After 1925 all adult males enjoyed the right to elect its members. The Japanese lower house lacked the power of budgetary control that might have made it the most effective instrument of government, for a constitutional provision stipulated that in any case of Diet refusal to pass a government appropriation, the previous year's budget should simply remain in effect. In addition, the Imperial prerogative gave the oligarchy an absolute veto over all Diet legislation.

Administrative functions of government belonged to the ministries, manned by professional bureaucrats and headed by members of the cabinet. From time to time the latter was a body of majority party leaders from the House of Representatives, but more often its membership depended on the choice of another fundamentally conservative body, the Privy Council, whose members held lifetime appointments from the Emperor. Still another advisory organ wielded much authority in the first quarter of the twentieth century. This was the genro, or elder statesmen, an extraconstitutional body of Satsuma or Chôshû clansmen (Itô, Yamagata, Inoue, Matsukata, Ôyama, and Katsura) plus the court noble, Prince Saionji.

Political parties in prewar Japan were originally liberal in purpose, since they were combinations of politicians out of power who wished to break the oligarchy's control. Later the oligarchs themselves saw the advantages to be gained by working through party organizations. In no case were parties unified around principles or coherent plans of action; all were directed by strong leaders, and new parties frequently came into being through bolts by politicians dissatisfied with their old alliances. On the whole, party government was never effectively realized. Promises that the two leading parties of the twenties might evolve a truly bipartisan government were dashed by the economic unrest and militarism of the thirties. As one cause, the ruling classes could never entirely dissociate the notion of an opposition party from disloyalty to the country. Radical parties continued to exist even under strong repression. The Social Democratic Party of the mid-thirties even managed to win thirty-seven Diet seats in the 1937 elections, while radical rightist groups such as that of Kita Ikki gave spiritual support to the frankly fascist domestic program of the extreme militarists. The small and illegal Japan Communist Party, founded in 1922, remained active through most of the 1920's with the constant infusion of new blood from among Moscow-trained revolutionaries but was forced into underground quiescence by the militarist repressions of the late twenties and thirties.

The above description applies to the forms Japanese were used to before 1945. The system was monolithic in a sense unfamiliar to Americans, for there were no autonomous local governments in which to experiment with the liberal novelties of women's suffrage, initiative and referendum, or toleration of radicals. The drawbacks of the system are obvious: it tended to concentrate power in the hands of a few venerables and keep it there; it tended to repress all progress toward liberalism or democracy; most disastrous of all, it allowed unbridled control of the civilian government by the least moderate elements in the military. The strong points are not so easy to see from our point of view, but they might be said to have included stability and encouragement (in early Meiji) of rapid achievement of military and industrial strength. In addition, the system took into account the public's lack of political experience and satisfied such urges to absolutism as Japan's Confucian and Shinto tradition produced.

Japan's present government rests on the foundation of the Constitution of 1947. This has been criticized as a wholly American document forced on an occupied country in no position to modify or reject it. To this it might be countered that Japan could probably have achieved a democratic constitution in no other way. Foremost of its innovations was the reduction of the emperor from absolute sovereign to mere symbol of state, who may not refuse the signature necessary to make Diet enactments into law. Accordingly, the new government was to be based on law before which all persons, even the emperor, were to be treated equally. The Constitution further provided for supremacy of the Diet as the legislative power, separation of powers—legislative, executive (the cabinet and ministries), and judicial (the courts)—and guarantees of popular liberties.

The Diet consists, as before, of two houses, but the House of Peers has been replaced by the wholly elected House of Councillors. The House of Representatives consists of 466 members elected from geographical districts. It is the stronger of the two houses, particularly in fiscal and foreign affairs. The prime minister and at least half of his cabinet must be chosen from its membership. The House of Councillors, with a membership of

250, includes members elected from the nation at large. Its powers are inferior to those of the lower house, which may kill bills it passes and may pass bills over its veto. On the other hand, the House of Representatives may be dissolved by the cabinet, forcing new elections, while councillors are elected to fixed terms of six years, and the upper house itself is not subject to dissolution.

The cabinet remains the principal executive organ in the government, much stronger than before, since the old Privy Council has been abolished. The eighteen cabinet members draft proposed legislation and submit it to the Diet, administer the executive ministries, supervise foreign relations, draw up a budget for Diet approval, and act on amnesties and commutations of punishment.

The twelve executive ministries are headed by cabinet members. Most are carry-overs from the prewar government. In keeping with the delegation of broad powers to local governments, the old Home Ministry, which administered the national police force and controlled prefectural assemblies, has been abolished. The old Ministry of Justice, which was in effect the judiciary arm of government, has been replaced by another ministry, the Attorney General's office, entrusted with the duties of a public prosecutor under an independent judiciary. Significant too is the innovation of a Ministry of Labor to enforce Japan's liberalized labor legislation. The extensive civil service, though largely employed by the ministries, is under a separate authority independent of cabinet control.

The new judiciary system is an independent branch of government equal in authority to the Diet and cabinet, whose decisions are subject to judicial review, as in the American legal system. The system consists of a Supreme Court, eight regional higher courts, district courts in each of the prefectures, and a number of summary courts. Family courts to adjudicate domestic complaints attest to the diminution of the power of family heads, once almost absolute, and the substitution for it of equal rights under law for all members of a family. A curious feature of the judiciary system is the provision that judges be reapproved by the people in the general elections following their appointment by the cabinet and at specified intervals thereafter. If a majority of voters favor the removal of a judge already appointed, he must be replaced. Furthermore, judges of the Supreme Court must be "learned persons of experience," and a certain number of them must be legal experts of at least twenty years' professional standing. Police powers have been removed completely from the judiciary as one of the first legal reforms designed to prevent Japan's age-old abuses resulting from concentration of legal power. As a deterrent to police brutality in criminal cases, confessions must be supported by other evidence.

No constitutional provision has been of more revolutionary impact than that disbanding armed forces and abolishing war "as an instrument of national policy." It was adopted in the hope that in the brave new postwar world it would be possible for a nation of Japan's strategic importance to remain the "Switzerland of the East," immune from attack because of her very defenselessness. In the succeeding cold war American policymakers soon realized that an impotent Japan would at best be a lasting burden on American defenses if she were to remain secure from communist aggression. Maintenance of United Nations troops in Japan during the Korean War in effect postponed the necessity of providing Japan permanent self-defense. A home defense force was instituted shortly before the conclusion of the peace treaty, but its existence poses a thorny constitutional problem. To date, the Constitution remains unamended, and most Japanese have expressed themselves at the polls as opposing immediate rearmament. The truly international nature of the defense problem is not yet fully realized in Japan.

Local government in Japan has been returned to the localities themselves, but there is no assurance that it will stay there. Mayors and governors of municipalities and prefectures are now elected directly by the people, as are local school boards. Local governments control school affairs, may levy emergency taxes, and have certain legislative powers. The efficiency of the local governments, particularly in regard to school boards, has been severely questioned of late. Certainly many local officials have lacked experience in government. In 1954 police affairs were returned to the control of the central government.

POLITICAL PARTIES

Before the war Japan's two leading political parties had been the *Seiyûkai* and *Minsei-tô*. With the revival of party government in the autumn of 1945, both reappeared to become the leading conservative parties, the former as the Liberal Party and the latter as the Progressive Party. Meanwhile, members of former proletarian parties organized the Japan Social Democratic Party, and the Communist Party came out of hiding with the return from exile or release from prison of its former leaders. A profusion of minor parties ranged from right to left behind candidates of widely varying backgrounds and degrees of political experience. In the 1946 general elections, 267 parties entered candidates. Since that time there has been an inevitable weeding out of most of the minor parties as well as splits or consolidations of the more vigorous of them.

Postwar political parties exhibit at least one of the striking characteristics of their prewar counterparts: they unify not so much around articulated programs or policies as behind dominating politicians. To be sure, there is a recognizable range of political sentiment in the parties that dominate the present political scene. Parties fall into two major classes roughly distinguishable as conservative and leftist, though these descriptions fail to note subtle points of unity and divergence not immediately appreciated by students of American political institutions. Following is a list of the principal parties active in national politics at the present time.

a. Conservative Groups. Three of Japan's major political factions and most of its minor ones are basically conservative in respect to the monarchy, private control of means of production and distribution, and alliance with the West. The minor conservative factions fulfill a useful democratic function in offering means of expression to dissidents from major parties; their best hope for exercise of power lies in coalition with one or more of the major groups. The major conservative factions are as follows:

1. The Liberal Party (*Jiyû-tô*): Majority Faction. The first postwar leader of the Liberals was Hatoyama Ichirô, who was purged in May, 1946. His successor, the present head of the party, is Prime Minister Yoshida Shigeru. Despite disaffections of some of its early leaders to the rival Progressives, the Liberals

have continued to be the stronger of the two groups. Few of its leaders were purged under the occupation compared with those of the Progressive Party. On winning an absolute majority of Diet seats in the January, 1949, elections, the Liberals attempted to form a united conservative front with the Progressives that has never materialized. As strongest single party in the government for the past five years, the Yoshida party has most notably favored acceptance of American military protection with a view to eventual building up of a self-sufficient defense force.

2. Liberal Party: Minority Faction. In the spring of 1953 a clash of personalities within the party precipitated a fall of the cabinet and new general elections. A dissident faction under the former party head, Hatoyama Ichirô, who had long since been freed from purge restrictions, opposed continued leadership of the party by the Prime Minister. Late in 1953 Hatoyama and some of his faction returned to the majority group, but a small number of others still remain outside it and are in effect a separate party. Similarity of program with the Yoshida Liberals would seem to make reconciliation with them desirable from the standpoint of both groups, though the personal animosities involved make this difficult to achieve.

3. Progressive Party (formerly *Minshu-tô,* or Democratic Party, and now officially *Kaishin-tô*). The present party leaders include Shigemitsu Mamoru and former Prime Minister Ashida Hitoshi (formerly of the Liberal Party). Here again differences from other conservative groups are more personal than doctrinal. (See footnote on p. 53.)

b. Socialist Parties. Since the war Japanese Socialists have formed nearly as heterogeneous and unstable a group as their conservative opponents. Early solidarity of the Social Democratic Party (*Shakai Minshu-tô*) led to an unexpected victory at the polls in April, 1947, followed by strong positions for the party in the two succeeding coalition cabinets under their own leader Katayama Tetsu as Prime Minister from June, 1947, until February, 1948, and under the Progressive Ashida as Premier for the next year to February, 1949. Fundamental differences between extremists and moderates within the party grew in the following period. In October, 1951, the two groups split.

1. Socialist Party (*Shakai-tô*): Right Wing. The immediate issue over which the Socialists split was Japanese ratification of a peace treaty in the drafting of which neither the Soviet Union nor China had participated. Right Wingers, though they opposed the U.S.–Japanese defense pact that accompanied the treaty, supported the treaty itself. This the Left Wingers refused to do. The Right Wing has since taken a firm stand against rearmament, at the same time avoiding the violent anti-Americanism of the Left Wing.

2. Socialist Party: Left Wing. The group that opposed Japanese ratification of both the peace treaty and the defense pact has maintained its strict opposition to cooperation with the West in all phases of its struggle with world communism. It opposed active and passive aid to the South Korean cause in the Korean War and favors complete withdrawal of all foreign defense troops from Japanese soil. At the same time, it staunchly resists rearmament for Japan either with or without amendment of the Constitution. Such a program attracts not only Japan's neutralists, to whom commitment on either side of the cold war seems ill-advised, but also those committed on the side of communism without being actually in the Communist Party.

(The suggestion is frequently made that Japanese political leaders make concerted efforts to adopt a two-party system using the existing major parties as a foundation. A consolidation of Liberals and Progressives into a single conservative party would not be too unwieldy a group from the standpoint of policy and would tend to give conservatives among the electorate more effective power than they have with the present unstable and faction-ridden political alignments. Moreover, such a coalition, if permanent, would doubtless encourage Right- and Left-Wing Socialists to patch up their differences and become more powerful spokesmen for Japanese liberalism. Defenders of the present multi-party setup point out that the provision for proportional representation in the House of Representatives makes it possible for splinter groups to find Diet expression for their opinions and that new coalitions would do little to prevent the personality clashes that are at the root of present factionalism.)

c. The Japan Communist Party (Nihon Kyôsan-tô). Communist strength in Japan cannot be gauged by its numerical strength in the Diet, which declined from a high of thirty-five representatives after the January, 1949, elections to its present low of one member in the lower house and none in the upper. In terms of its discipline, its hidden external support by Russia and the international party organization and its potential appeal in times of crisis to possible millions not now swayed by its program, the Japan Communist Party must be considered one of the major parties. Its avowed aims include immediate withdrawal of U.S. security forces, abrogation of the U.S.–Japanese defense pact, and continued disarmament, abolition of the monarchy, and social reforms. Incorporation of Japan into the communist bloc of nations is an ultimate aim.

During the occupation years the party offered a program of so-called peaceful revolution, designed to build popular support and at the same time ward off the wrath of the occupying authorities that would have resulted from a more overtly revolutionary policy. In consequence, orders from Moscow in January, 1950, purged top Japanese party officials, replacing them with others who supported more radical methods. Purge from the opposite direction in July, 1950, followed the outbreak of the Korean War. The party's official newspaper, the *Akahata,* was forced to suspend publication at the same time that other measures were taken by the occupation to prevent Communist obstruction of the United Nations war effort. Since the peace treaty became effective in April, 1952, the party has again enjoyed the legal status of all other parties.

Composition of the House of Representatives, by parties, as of December 1, 1953, was as follows:

Liberal Party: Majority Faction	222
Liberal Party: Minority Faction	13
Progressive Party *	76
Socialist Party: Right Wing	66
Socialist Party: Left Wing	71
Communist Party	1
Other parties	13
Independents	2
Vacancies	2
Total	466

* Late in November, 1954, the Progressives under Shigemitsu Mamoru combined with anti-Yoshida elements in the Liberal Party and other splinter groups in the Diet to form a new party known as the Japan Democratic Party (*Nihon Minshu-tô*) under the leadership of Hatoyama Ichirô. At the time of its organization the party numbered 121, reducing the Liberal strength in the Diet from 222 to an estimated 185.

ADINGS

ischauer, Robert Karl. *Japan, Government—Politics.* New York, Thomas Nelson, 1939.

Scalapino, Robert A. *Democracy and the Party Movement in Prewar Japan; the Failure of the First Attempt.* Berkeley and Los Angeles, University of California Press, 1953.

Swearingen, Rodger, and Paul Langer. *Red Flag in Japan; International Communism in Action, 1919–1951.* Cambridge, Harvard University Press, 1952.

ECONOMIC LIFE

In terms of agricultural land the population of Japan is the densest of any country in the world. The natural deficiency of raw materials resulting from overpopulation is aggravated by the near absence of several materials essential to the maintenance of a highly developed industrial economy. Wartime destruction or deterioration of industrial, agricultural, and conservation facilities further complicates the nation's essentially weak economic condition, making her more than ever before dependent on foreign trade and the economic stability of her Asian and trans-Pacific neighbors. Ultimately, then, solution of the economic problems facing Japan today depends partly on international conditions over which the Japanese themselves have no control. The present survey of Japan's economic life, although expressed largely in terms of material supplies, industrial capacity, and demands for finished goods, cannot be fully appraised without reference to several factors of a more or less political nature. Two such factors are the relations between Japan and the Communist-dominated areas of continental Asia and the demands by the countries of southeast Asia for reparations to be used in the reconstruction of their battered economy. Among the other influences on Japan's economy that cannot be discussed solely in economic terms are British and American tariff protection against competition from Japanese goods and the latent threat to the Japanese economy of the still untapped industrial resources of Asia at large.

Economic solutions, if solutions are to be found, must be sought in the natural advantages that Japan possesses and that keep shortages from being still more oppressive:

1. Japan's climate is on the whole favorable to intensive cropping, as rainfall is plentiful and winters (except in Hokkaido and northern Honshu) mild enough to permit two crops annually. Uplands unsuited to the cultivation of rice provide most other foods and timber.

2. The high level of Japanese industrial development permits her a lucrative export trade in goods such as cotton textiles, which are processed in Japan from raw materials imported from other parts of the world.

3. Export commodities such as watches, cameras, and precision instruments are excellently suited to the natural limitations of the Japanese economy, since they involve a negligible drain on scarce raw materials and at the same time offer an outlet for skilled labor and advanced manufacturing techniques.

4. Despite wartime losses, industrial reconstruction has been rapid, particularly in the last three or four years. The industrial production index, computed on the basis of an average of 100 for the years 1934–36, was only 78.2 for 1949; by July, 1953, it had risen to 168.

NATURAL RESOURCES

The process of national modernization that created a demand in Japan for overseas resources also enabled her to bid for a self-sufficient network of colonial dependencies on the mainland through militarism and power politics. The prewar Japanese Empire was never entirely self-sufficient, but it was relatively so in foodstuffs and hence incomparably more secure economically than the shorn homeland of today. Japan is now self-sufficient in few of the materials necessary for her survival, while, on the other hand, her potential supply of luxury commodities such as tea and silk has become far too great for the dwindling international demand.

Of essential mineral resources only sulphur is produced in quantity adequate to the domestic demand. The most serious mineral deficiency is in iron, of which Japanese mines yield about 1,000,000 tons a year, 20 percent of her annual consumption. Total reserves are only 80,000,000 tons, half of it low-grade ore.

Coal deposits come close to satisfying the nation's present consumption rate (43,000,000 tons in 1952), but native coal is of too poor a quality for coking purposes, is inferior in calorific value to that found in the United States, and, because it is found in narrow seams with frequent offsets, is expensive to mine. In addition, reserves are low—220 metric tons per capita, as opposed to 27,000 metric tons in the United States and 4,200 metric tons in England.

The 74,000 metric tons of copper produced annually at the present time are nearly sufficient for domestic needs. In addition, Japan is self-sufficient or nearly so in gold, silver, and chromite.

Petroleum reserves are limited to northern Japan and are very low. At present they produce about 350,000 kiloliters of crude oil a year as against imports of 5,000,000 kiloliters.

Annual imports of other minerals are an index of their scarcity in Japan. Principal of these are manganese ore (160,000

metric tons imported annually, 50 percent of the national consumption), zinc ore (10,000 metric tons, 10 percent), and salt,
which is produced by the evaporation of sea water but which is
relatively scarce, since the heavy rainfall in most areas hinders
solar evaporation (1,500,000 metric tons imported annually,
80 percent of the yearly consumption). Mineral demands that
must be satisfied almost entirely from overseas supplies include
bauxite (160,000 metric tons imported annually), phosphate
rock (1,000,000 metric tons), and potash (180,000 metric tons).

Japan's mountainous topography and heavy precipitation
offer her a large potential supply of cheap hydroelectric power,
if one ignores the heavy cost of installing dams, power stations,
and transmission lines. Over 40,000,000,000 kilowatt-hours were
generated by Japanese water power plants in 1952, about 80 percent of the total for all power sources. (The electric power supply
for the United States is about eight times the Japanese total.)
More dams and reservoirs are needed to guarantee an even
flow of hydroelectric power throughout the months when generation capacity is low.

AGRICULTURE

Three considerations have imposed on Japanese agriculture most
of its essential features. The climate—temperate, rainy, and with
a relatively long growing season in much of the country—is on
the whole well suited to varied and efficient crop production
(though destructive floods are not uncommon); the land, where
arable at all, is not of the highest fertility and requires much
fertilization; human ingenuity has done much to make use of
natural advantages and to overcome inherent disadvantages

through intensive farming. Among the devices in use are terracing of upland fields for the increase of arable land, construction of dikes around rice paddies, constant weeding, fertilization, watering, and double cropping.

The total land in Japan suitable for cultivation is only about 16,000,000 acres, little more than one sixth the total land area. Even this figure represents a great achievement by the government and the farmers during the Meiji and Taishô periods, for nearly a third of it is land made usable at great cost by draining marshes, terracing slopes, and clearing forests. Little reclamation was accomplished between 1921 and 1945, though a new campaign was undertaken after the Second World War to bring more marginal land under cultivation. Recent figures show that the 1945 total had been increased by somewhat more than 1,000,000 acres. Prospects are dim for appreciable additional reclamation, since what has been accomplished to date has nearly exhausted the supply of marginal land.

Of the total arable acreage more than half is used to produce the annual rice crop of about 600,000,000 bushels. This utilization of virtually all lowland area for the production of one crop is a natural accommodation to geographic limitations, for only rice yields so many calories per unit of land. Rice cultivation in Japan is highly efficient, yielding two to three times as much per acre as in the major rice-producing nations of continental Asia. Other grains, principally wheat and barley, supplement rice at meals but are never considered substitutes for it. Sweet and white potatoes complete the list of staple foods. Production of all staples has increased gradually since the end of the war but has not yet equaled the peak yield of 1939. Since the population has increased by about 20 percent since that time, the real food supply has deteriorated still further than absolute figures show.

A widespread practice for increasing the productivity of land is the harvesting of two or more crops a year from one field. In the case of rice land, the second crop is usually a winter crop such as wheat or barley. From 30 to 40 percent of the irrigated rice land in the country is farmed in this fashion, and the area harvested is thereby increased by about one third.

Fertilizers are of two kinds, natural and chemical. The use of night soil as the basic fertilizer is characteristic of Japanese farming, as it is of agriculture on the Asiatic mainland. In addition, green manure, compost, wood ashes, bean cake, and fish fertilizers are used. Natural fertilizers are customarily mixed with water and allowed to decompose in concrete cisterns. For economy the liquid fertilizer thus produced is applied directly to growing plants rather than being spread evenly over entire fields. In recent decades Japan has developed a large chemical fertilizer industry, and despite serious wartime setbacks, production has made rapid strides toward recovery of prewar norms. The 1952 production total for commercial fertilizers was two thirds of the prewar high.

Livestock is naturally in short supply because of the scarcity of good pasture land. It is estimated that there are 2,300,000 cattle, 1,100,000 horses, and 1,000,000 hogs in Japan. Two- to threefold increases in the number of goats and sheep since the war have brought the number to a mere 450,000 for the former and 325,000 for the latter. In the absence of farm mechanization, cattle must be used primarily as draft animals, further reducing the quantity of livestock available for food.

Collapse of the international demand for Japanese tea and

silk has severely crippled the nation's two principal non-food crop industries. Tea is down two fifths from the prewar high of 125,000,000 pounds a year. Synthetic fibers such as rayon and nylon have caused the annual production of silk to fall to about one third of the prewar peak of 87,000,000 pounds. Japan can ill afford to increase the production of silk much beyond the overseas demand for it, since silkworm culture entails a sacrifice to mulberries of arable land otherwise available for food crops. Japan's other important fiber crops are hemp, cotton, flax, jute, and ramie, but the total output of these goods is far short of the domestic demand. Tobacco is grown in moderate quantity and is processed and marketed under government monopoly. Imports make up for domestic deficiencies.

The intensive nature of Japanese farming and the plentiful supply of farm labor have made extensive use of labor-saving devices both impractical and unnecessary. Such motorized implements as irrigation pumps, hullers, and threshers have been in increasingly common use since the war, but heavy equipment—tractor-driven plows, for example—is still all but unknown.

Before the war the ownership of farm land tended to be concentrated. Of all farmers, 27 percent owned no land at all, 42 percent owned only part of the land they cultivated, and only 31 percent owned their own farms. Land rents were high, fertilizer and equipment expensive. Net incomes as low as 30 percent of the value of harvested crops were common. The extreme poverty resulting from such a situation led most farm families to subsidiary occupations. Beginning in 1946 the Allied occupation sponsored legislation designed to reduce tenant farming and improve the condition of farmers remaining in a tenant status. All land owned by absentee landlords was put up for resale; resident landlords might keep 2.5 acres of tenant-farmed land (10 acres in Hokkaido); the government paid former landowners in annuity bonds and resold property to farmers in installments over a maximum of thirty years. In addition, rents were limited by law to cash, not to exceed 25 percent of the value of the rice crop and 15 percent of the value of other crops. Written contracts of tenancy were made obligatory, and the form of such contracts was standardized to eliminate long-standing abuses of insecure tenancy from which farmers previously suffered. As a result of the occupation's land reform program, 4,500,000 acres of land had been sold to the farmers by 1951, reducing the area of tenant-farmed land from 6,300,000 acres to 1,670,000 acres. The social impact of this revolutionary program is impossible to measure, but it is safe to say that by greatly improving the farmers' lot in an agricultural country, it should have a considerable stabilizing effect on Japanese society as a whole.

The government has encouraged farm cooperatives since early in the present century. Occupation-sponsored legislation standardized operating procedure and permitted farm cooperatives to engage in virtually all kinds of economic activity. By 1948 cooperatives handled 36 percent of all farm purchases, 61 percent of farmer sales, 64 percent of financial deposits, and 71 percent of loans to farmers.

Japan's greatest agricultural problems are rooted not in the inefficiencies of man-made systems or institutions but in the inequities of nature that impoverish all phases of the nation's economic life. Productivity per acre of cultivated land is already much higher than in most other countries, but it must be still greater if the farm population is to improve its low standard of living. Solution may come partly through scientific or technical improvements such as are being studied in the government's several hundred agricultural research stations. Full solution of the agrarian problem can come, however, only through increased industrialization and more foreign trade.

FORESTRY AND FISHERIES

About two thirds of Japan's land area is forested. Lumber is the predominant building material; charcoal and charcoal gas are the principal fuels. Consumption of wood for these purposes and for others including paper manufacture averaged 2,600,000,000 cubic feet a year from 1930 to 1934. The difference between this figure and the annual growth rate of 1,600,000,000 cubic feet must be compensated for by imports or by gradual depletion of timber resources. Loss to the Soviet Union of southern Sakhalin, which was an important prewar source of lumber and pulp, complicates the problem.

The fishing industry is a natural source of food in a country where pasture land is a luxury. The average Japanese eats about sixty-five pounds of fish, but only five pounds of meat, per year. (Average figures for the United States are 12 pounds of fish and 140 pounds of meat.) Wartime losses have brought about unprecedented shortages of marine products. Intensive use of nearby waters has gradually depleted the supply of fish within easy access to Japanese ports. Moreover, international agreements restrict Japanese fishing boats to a comparatively small area between the International Date Line and the middle of the Japan Sea. Lack of sufficient fishing craft has further contributed to the reduction of the prewar catch of 7,000,000 tons a year to about half that figure.

INDUSTRY

Little more than eighty years ago the Japanese government launched an industrialization campaign such as no other modern nation has equaled. Handicapped by an essentially weak economy, Japan had few advantages in its struggle to obtain equality with Western nations except unlimited man-power and the willingness and capacity to borrow wholesale whatever techniques were necessary to complete the job. Though the campaign was successful, the gain was slight to those whose toil made success possible. Seventy years of indus-trial development made Japan a first-rate military and naval power and a commercial force to be reckoned with but did less than might have been expected to improve the standard of living of the majority of the Japanese people. Manufacture of con-sumer goods lagged consistently behind defense industry, and production of goods for home consumption ran far short of export manufactures. Meanwhile, industrial slums grew, rank-ing with the world's most unwholesome. It is a major postwar irony that with factories free for the first time to concentrate on consumer goods, the average Japanese consumer cannot afford to buy such goods, nor can sufficient markets be found for them overseas.

The bulk of Japanese industrial enterprises operate with fewer than five workers. Such plants are survivals from the ancient domestic craft system, which traditionally produced the tools, the clothing, and the agricultural products necessary even under a self-sufficient agrarian economy. Organized in guilds and operating through a spiraling network of middlemen, financiers, and distributors, such shops still produce most of the country's processed foods, textiles, ceramics, and wood products. In many cases, mechanized industries have continued to operate under the shop system. Some small textile factories, for example, use power looms.

Factory industry flourished under militaristic government and high finance capital. Though the textile industry has always employed more workers than any other branch of Japanese industry, the classes of manufacturing which grew most conspicuously in the decade or so before the war were those directly or indirectly connected with Japan's expanding military machine—ships, aircraft, motor vehicles, munitions, communications equipment, and machine tools, for example. Industry for nonmilitary purposes had never been much more than adequate; yet with industrial mobilization before and during the Pacific war, it was forced to give way still further to increasing military demands. From 1940 to 1944 consumer expenditures declined by 30 percent. It was not until the latter year that war industry reached its peak productivity. After that time the advance of the Allied Forces blocked off overseas sources of raw materials, while bombing of Japanese factories further crippled industrial output. Just one year after reaching its peak, Japanese industrial output had fallen by July, 1945, to 40 percent of that figure.

The main problem facing postwar Japanese industry was that of physical reconstruction. In view of the collapse of the over-all national economy, the problem could be expressed as essentially one of financing. Until 1949 uncontrolled inflation tended to dissipate much of the funds appropriated for rebuilding. A government agency, the Reconstruction Finance Bank, came to the aid of industries unable to provide the necessary capital for their own reconstruction. Concerted efforts by the Japanese government and the occupation to bring the inflation under control finally speeded up the reconstruction process so that by 1950 the index of industrial production actually exceeded the average for 1934–36 (102.9 as against a base of 100 for those years). The index for July, 1953, was 168.

Foreign demands for Japanese export goods largely determine the types of products on which Japan's industry concentrates. Decline in overseas demand for Japanese textiles has reduced the proportional monetary value of exports of these goods from 52 percent of all exports in 1934–36 to 35 percent in 1952. Heavy industry has become more important with the increased demand for partially manufactured goods in Asiatic countries that are becoming industrialized. Metal and metal products now account for 27 percent of all exports, more than twice the prewar proportion. An additional 9 percent of all exports consists of ships, automobiles, rolling stock, sewing machines, textile machinery, machine parts, and other machinery. This represents a slight increase, both in absolute figures and proportionally to total exports, over prewar machinery production. Further expansion would be highly desirable but is impeded by lack of overseas markets. Japan is the only machinery-supplying country in Asia and stands to gain from the expanding industrialization programs of the south Asian countries. Even so, the growth in demand for Japanese goods in these areas hardly compensates for the loss of the important prewar market in the nearby mainland.

Many problems have beset postwar Japanese industry. The fundamental one of reconstruction has already been mentioned; others include the following: (1) the growth in importance of heavy industry, necessitating modernization of equipment and methods of production and forcing increased importation of bulky, expensive-to-ship raw materials; (2) conversion of former industries to the production of consumer goods (the shift was, of course, of benefit to the economy as a whole); (3) uncertainties as to the extent of plant and goods confiscation for reparations; the Allies originally contemplated much more extensive stripping of Japan's industrial potential than was finally agreed upon; (4) collapse of the international commercial system by which prewar Japan had obtained raw materials and found markets for processed goods; (5) deconcentration of industries by the occupation, which made for diminished over-all efficiency of production; and (6) removal of trained managers from control of industries under the occupation's purge restrictions. Some of these problems made for no more than temporary setbacks in industrial productivity, while others, for example, the loss of mainland sources of raw materials, remain perplexing ones.

FINANCE

The present-day currency and banking systems have evolved from those set up under the Meiji government from forty to eighty-five years ago. Several of the largest modern banking houses, established as goods wholesalers and merchant banks long before the Meiji period, were permitted by the early Meiji government to issue their own notes convertible to gold or silver and up to 150 percent of the banks' specie holdings. Ten years of mildly regulated private banking led to the disappearance of much gold and widespread inflation in the train of which the government in the early 1880's undertook a series of measures designed to bring financial institutions and the national currency under closer supervision. A central bank, The Bank of Japan, was set up as a repository for specie holdings of national banks, sole issuer of banknotes (the old notes of nationally chartered private banks were withdrawn), and general fiscal agent for the government. The government commenced the chartering of ordinary banks, whose minimum capitalization came in time to be regulated by law. The currency system from this period on functioned efficiently and stably, though the demands of a wartime economy forced 1942 revisions in the direction of stricter control by the Ministry of Finance, and the postwar economic collapse made the operation of the fiscal machinery completely ineffective for several years.

The government has from time to time established other public banks for specialized financing. Among these the Hypothec Bank for agricultural development and the Industrial Bank still operate. Others now defunct existed for colonial development and the financing of wartime industry.

A striking feature of the prewar economy was the concentration of private capital in a few large combines, the zaibatsu firms, all of them under the hereditary control of what was virtually a finance caste. The fifteen largest of these, including the Mitsui, Mitsubishi, Sumitomo, and Yasuda combines, are estimated to have accounted for three quarters of Japan's prewar business transactions. Companies in zaibatsu hands were not limited to heavy and light manufacturing concerns but included shipping, wholesale, retail, and warehouse firms; banks; insurance companies; trust companies; and real estate concerns. By forcing the sale on the open market of shares in the hands of zaibatsu families, the occupation aimed at freeing fiscal management from the control of a clique that had in the past been too easily manipulated to the purposes of a militarist and expansionist oligarchy.

TRANSPORTATION AND COMMUNICATIONS

Japan has 18,600 miles of railroad track (compared with 225,800 in the United States). Of this, 14,000 miles are government owned. Trackage per unit area compares roughly with that in other densely populated regions of the world such as England and western Europe. Revenue from passenger service exceeds that from freight shipment, due in part to the ease of coastal freight shipment to most of the country's heavily populated areas.

Coastal shipping is privately managed, though subject to government regulation. Wartime losses of ships caused a temporary diversion of goods normally shipped coastwise to the railroads, which were ill-equipped to handle them. Subsidies to shipowners have been necessary in order to enable them to compete with the publicly owned railroads.

The prewar merchant marine ranked third in the world, after those of Britain and the United States. Mobilized during the war, it was practically annihilated by the end of it. Of a prewar total of 6,000,000 tons of vessels 100 gross tons or over, only 1,400,000 tons remained, much of this unserviceable. By the end of March, 1953, the gross tonnage had been increased to

2,850,000. Construction of new ships had been rapid, and the situation continues to improve. Removal of hampering occupation restrictions on overseas shipping and return of lines, which had been government-managed since the war, to private control (1950) have been further encouragements to this vital element in Japanese commerce.

The prewar Japan Airways Company was a partly government-owned monopoly. All Japanese aviation was prohibited by the occupation, and only in 1952 did a domestic civil airline reappear (trans-Pacific service was inaugurated in 1954).

Highways are poor compared with those of other industrialized countries and are far less important to the transportation picture than the railroads. Only about 1 percent of the total mileage (664,000 miles) in 1947 was paved. In 1949 there were fewer than 300,000 motor vehicles registered, of which over two thirds were trucks.

Telephone and telegraph services are government monopolies, both of them struggling to recover from the extensive damage suffered during the war. Of 1,500,000 telephones in 1940, only 800,000 were in operation in 1945. By 1949 most had been restored, though there were still fewer than one fifteenth the number per capita in the United States. Telegraphy is a more important means of communication; the postwar monthly average of telegrams exceeds 5,000,000.

The prewar government monopoly of radio broadcasting by the Japan Broadcasting Company (NHK) was brought to an end recently with the licensing of private stations, although the occupation had removed the NHK itself from direct supervision of the Ministry of Communications. Television broadcasting was inaugurated in 1953.

Industrialized Japan depends utterly on foreign trade, both to supply her with the raw materials that she lacks and as an outlet for the processed goods whose manufacture is the indispensable supplement to the inherently impoverished domestic economy. Internal commerce must not be overlooked in any appraisal of the total national economy, however, as it has always outweighed foreign trade in quantity and in the number of individuals involved.

Industrial items now account for the overwhelming majority of Japanese exports. By kinds of products, 53 percent are fully manufactured goods, 35 percent semi-manufactures, 8 percent foodstuffs, 3 percent raw materials, and 1 percent miscellaneous (1952 figures). Textiles are still the most important single group of export commodities (35 percent), followed by metals and metal goods (27 percent), machinery (9 percent), foodstuffs (8 percent), ceramics and glassware (4 percent), and chemicals (3 percent). Other export commodities include paper, clocks and watches, toys, and optical instruments. The total dollar value for 1952 of Japanese export goods was $1,273,000,000 as against the average figure for 1932–36 (adjusted to 1951 dollar prices) of $1,652,000,000.

Imports cost Japan about $2,000,000,000 in 1952. This was a substantial increase over the 1932–36 figure ($1,705,000,000, adjusted as above). Of total imports, 32 percent were foods and 29 percent raw materials for textiles. The great cotton spinning industry depends almost entirely on foreign sources for raw cotton. In 1952, 1,993,000 bales of cotton were imported, nearly 45 percent of it from the United States. Other imports include iron ore, coal, petroleum, machinery, crude rubber, chemicals, raw materials for fertilizer, fats and oils, salt, and raw hides.

Prewar Japan derived 42 percent of her export income from China, Korea, and Formosa. In 1952, on the other hand, the same areas bought only 8 percent of Japan's exports. At present Great Britain and other sterling areas provide Japan with her largest market ($612,000,000 out of a total [F.O.B.] of $1,581,000,000 for 1951), with the United States ($417,000,000), Canada ($14,000,000), other Far Eastern areas ($325,000,000), Latin America ($89,000,000), and Europe ($88,000,000) other major customers. (Figures include special procurement by foreign forces.) Figures for 1952 showed a sudden marked decline in exports to southeast Asia due in part to the postwar recovery of British and German markets in the area and in part to the tightening of sterling exchange restrictions. The tendency for most of Japan's customers is to import less and less finished light industry products and more and more products of heavy industry, that is, producer goods. Exports to the United States and Europe, however, are largely of the consumer goods category, many of them semiluxury goods, the demand for which would not be maintained in case of a full-scale recession in those countries.

Since the war, import sources have changed in much the same way as export destinations. Continental Asia, which once provided over half of all imports to Japan, now sends barely a quarter. Imports from North America, on the other hand, have increased from 25 percent to 50 percent of the total from all areas. In 1951 sources for imports were headed by the United States ($692,000,000 [C.I.F.] of a total of $1,995,000,000), the sterling areas ($452,000,000), Latin America ($260,000,000),

the Far East ($248,000,000), Europe ($125,000,000), the Middle
East ($112,000,000), and Canada ($14,000,000).

In discussing Japan's international balance of trade, it is
necessary to make a clear distinction between visible and invisible trade. Invisible trade includes services, capital transactions, and donations. So far as visible trade is concerned,
Japan's deficit has mounted year after year since the end of the
war. Causes for the imbalance have been decrease in productive
capacity for export goods, greater demand for imported foods
and reconstruction materials, increased shipment charges due
to the destruction of Japanese vessels, and loss of cheap supply
sources in the former colonies. From 1945 to 1952 the total
excess of import payments over export receipts was
$1,752,000,000. The invisible trade balance (exclusive of United
States foreign aid payments) likewise showed a deficit for Japan
from 1945 to 1949. Since 1950, however, there has been a sharp
reversal of the trend due to large-scale dollar receipts in so-called
special procurement transactions, that is, the supplying of goods
and services to United States and United Nations troops and
personnel in Japan and Korea. As a result, by the end of 1952
Japan had an aggregate invisible trade credit of $785,000,000.
During the same period (1945–52) United States aid to Japan
totaled $2,111,000,000, making a total credit of all postwar inter-
national payments of $1,144,000,000. It is obvious from these
figures that Japan cannot at the present rate maintain solvency
on the basis of visible trade alone. On the other hand, the advantageous balance of invisible trade has depended on the temporary accident of Japan's purveyor role in the Korean War. The
enormous drain on the United States treasury of dollar aid to
Japan cannot be expected to continue indefinitely. Nonessential

imports have already been all but eliminated by legislative controls. Monotonously, the only solution seems to be increased export trade.

Japanese foreign trade is beset by many problems over which Japan herself has very little control. Related to the trade imbalance described above is the problem of currency inconvertibility. Before the war, excesses of imports from specific areas could be compensated for by excesses of exports in others, since foreign currencies were at that time freely convertible. With the division of most of the free world into economic blocs (none of them including Japan), imbalances in Japan's trade with any one bloc must be remedied entirely by adjustment of that bloc's account. Some sort of Pacific Payments Union, similar to the European Payments Union, which helped free trade in Europe, would help Japan to avoid the simultaneous accumulations of debts to some areas and credits from others.

Other problems stem from the recent revolution in the world textile market. For her former pre-eminence in the silk trade, Japan is now attempting to substitute a growing export cotton industry. As Japan's cotton supply is negligible, she must buy abroad the raw cotton she processes, mainly from the United States, Pakistan, and Mexico. From the standpoint of Japanese economics, the industry is ideal: it affords outlets for labor, techniques, and merchant marine facilities, which Japan has; but it is not a drain on raw materials, which she lacks. Yet from the world economic standpoint the cotton trade is precarious, for it depends on two conditions that make for economic hardship and inefficiency elsewhere. The first of these conditions is the low state of industrialization in the rest of Asia; it would certainly be more desirable for Pakistan, as an example, if she were in a position to process her own cotton for consumption by her own people, a development, in fact, that India has already begun. The second condition is the relative cheapness of Japanese labor over that of the British Isles; if labor costs were equal, a cotton trade wholly between sterling bloc countries would be more advantageous to those countries than one involving Japan.

Related to the question of cheap Japanese labor is the recurring problem of foreign tariffs. In some instances Japan's interests compete directly with those of Britain and the United States, for example, in the textile and canned goods industries. Tariffs are maintained in advanced industrial countries on the plea of high labor costs and in the interest of internal economy. On the other hand, the entire free world has a political interest in Japanese economic security; further impoverishment of Japan could not possibly be to the political advantage of any Western country.

More vexing still is the problem of trade with China. Prewar Japan sent one third of her exports to and derived one sixth of her imports from China and Manchuria. Furthermore, many of the commodities Japan formerly derived from China were bulky goods—salt, soybeans, iron ore, coal, for example—which must now be transported at much higher cost from more distant sources. There is no question that revival of full-scale trade between the two countries would be an economic boon to Japan. Trade overtures from the Chinese Communists indicate an eagerness on their part to obtain Japanese products, but it should not be assumed that revival of the China trade would be easy to accomplish on terms satisfactory to Japan nor that it would solve all of Japan's economic problems. For one thing, increasing industrialization in Communist China has created a greater demand in China itself for the raw materials that Japan would like to buy there. Moreover, the export products that Japan could most efficiently supply are precisely those consumer goods which the Communist government will not permit its citizenry to import. The need in China is for products of heavy industry, that is, producer goods, and these would not only be difficult for the Japanese economy to send in large quantity but would add further urgency to the political question that underlies the whole issue: Is it advisable for Japan to lend her economic support to the strengthening of the Chinese Communist state, which has already shown itself to be politically antagonistic, expansionist, and of frightening economic potentialities?

LABOR

One of the most significant developments in Japanese economic life since the Second World War has been the rise of a virile labor movement, which by 1950 reached a total of seven million members. Unions existed in pre-war Japan under strong company supervision; by 1940, however, even these were virtually nonexistent. The occupation sought to foster a free labor movement, emphasizing American goals of safety legislation, collective bargaining, and mediation procedures. By the early months of 1947, under the leadership of the leftist National Congress of Industrial Unions, labor had participated directly in political activities and a general strike was prevented only by the last-minute, personal intervention of General Mac-Arthur. During the next year, the labor movement was largely

successful in resisting Communist infiltration and a Labor
Ministry was established as a new and important branch of
the national government. The labor movement in general has
taken a strongly neutral attitude on international problems and
has consistently opposed recent trends toward conservatism
and reaction at home.

READINGS

Cohen, Jerome B. *The Japanese Economy in War and Reconstruction*. Foreword by Sir George Sansom. Minneapolis, University
of Minnesota Press, 1949.

The following serials and periodicals may be found useful in supplying news and statistics on current economic matters:

Bank of Japan. *Economic Statistics of Japan,* annual. Tokyo, Bank
of Japan, 1925——.
Bank of Japan. *Quarterly Review*. Tokyo, Bank of Japan, 1948——.
Journal of Finance and Commerce, monthly. Tokyo, Nippon
Times, 1948——.
Mitsubishi Economic Research Bureau. *Monthly Circular. Analyti-
cal and Statistical Survey of Economic Conditions in Japan.*
Tokyo, 1–210, 1924–41; 211——, 1947——.
The Oriental Economist, monthly. Tokyo, The Oriental Economist,
1934——.

FILMS

Farmers of Japan. Department of Agriculture, U.S. Government,
Washington, D.C.
Japan, 80 Million Mouths to Feed. Encyclopaedia Britannica Films,
1150 Wilmette Ave., Wilmette, Ill.

SOCIAL AND CULTURAL LIFE

RACIAL ORIGINS

The physical characteristics of the Japanese people most closely resemble those of the Mongoloid race of China and northeast Asia. Mongoloid features present in most Japanese include straight black hair, dark-brown eyes, the "slant-eyed" appearance of the fold in the eyelids at the inner canthus, low nasal bridge, yellowish-brown skin, and the Mongoloid spot found at the base of the spine of many new-born infants. However, certain common features differ from those of other Mongoloids. Strains of the Caucasoid Ainus may account for the relative hairiness of Japanese among Mongoloid peoples, although numbers of wavy-haired Japanese presumably derive from an admixture of southern Asiatic stock. In addition, Japanese are typically shorter than North Chinese and Mongolians, averaging (for men) five feet five inches.

Archaeology too indicates a north Asiatic origin for some of the ancestors of the modern Japanese. Cultural anthropologists find it significant, however, that certain culture traits—in mythology and domestic architecture, for example—resemble those of Malaysia and Polynesia and are quite dissimilar from those of China and Korea.

SOME ASPECTS OF THE NATIONAL CHARACTER

Time has blended the strains from which the Japanese race has descended into a homogeneous nation. There is a danger in speaking of the national traits of any people, but if one grants from the start that individual exceptions exist in plenty to every rule of Japanese behavior, certain meaningful generalizations remain. The Japanese display strong national pride and sensitivity; they are given both to undue chauvinism for national achievements and to painful embarrassment at what they conceive to be national shortcomings. More positively, they are genuinely concerned with the interests of their whole society, placing them before family interests or the advantage of provinces or classes.

Dishonesty is not characteristic of the Japanese. "Polite lies" have a place in the deportment of all nations; the Japanese resort to them in social situations where the expression of a flatly contradictory opinion would be considered intolerable rudeness. To Americans, whose social usages prescribe a greater degree of frankness and directness, such evasions sometimes inspire an unjustified distrust of Japanese sincerity. In fact, some national practices indicate personal honesty and scrupulousness to the letter of the law greater than in our own culture. Houses are generally left unlocked at all times and, in the absence of coined money, one makes pay-station telephone calls on the honor system, depositing bills in boxes supplied beside the phone.

The Japanese dislike intensely the embarrassments of personal rebuff and confessions of failure and employ many devices to avoid causing or receiving loss of face. Among them is the extensive use of go-betweens in business and social relations.

Many observers have pointed out a dominant aesthetic sense in the Japanese temperament. Universal appreciation and preservation of the natural beauty of their homeland and a love of aesthetically pleasing pastimes (flower viewing, flower arranging, the tea ceremony, for instance) are striking instances of this. In addition, they maintain traditions of fine style in the manufacture of everyday utilitarian objects.

Most of the components of traditional Japanese higher culture have their origins in Korea or China. Early contacts with China brought Japan directly out of the stone age and gave her the rudiments of her art, industry, and government. Even indigenous institutions, such as the native religion and the Imperial House, were profoundly modified by contact with Chinese counterparts. Yet the insularity of the Japanese always prevented their civilization from becoming identical with that of the Continent. Modern Chinese and Japanese civilizations illustrate the possibility of wide divergence from a single cultural background.

The westernization of Japan has seemingly touched all phases of the national life. Rapid transportation and communications, machine industry, and the study of fascism, socialism, and democratic liberalism have had profound effects on national habits. The cultivation of Western dress, music, and amusements are more superficial aspects of the same process. Naturally, much remains that is characteristically oriental, and this will doubtless modify whatever Western traits become naturalized.

The Japanese have been characterized, usually contemptuously, as an "imitative" people. Certainly they have been successful in adapting to their own purposes traits from many different cultures. On the other hand, there are elements in every department of their civilization that have no exact equivalents in any other country: the classic drama and poetic forms in literature, a cuisine making distinctive use of sea foods, a native sect—that of Nichiren—within the Buddhist faith, even inventions and technological advances based on Western scientific knowledge. It would be more accurate to say that Japanese civilization, neither unique nor indigenous, has hitherto been part of the civilization of East Asia and that it is now perhaps responding to new challenges by becoming part of a new Pacific civilization. Japan has used whatever the other parts of those civilizations had to offer in the way of material and ideological advances, and in her turn has contributed inventions and ideas of her own to them. Some Japanese, it is true, are faddists. In the history of Japanese fashion, these have imitated everything from Chinese prose poems to left-bank novels and from Hindu musical instruments to pinball machines. Genuine assimilation of foreign culture, however, is another matter entirely. It has been a major aspect of the extraordinary vitality and adaptability of Japanese civilization.

SOCIAL CLASSES

It is common for foreigners to suppose that there are by and large two classes of Japanese society—rich and poor. There is in fact an important middle class in the small businesses and the professions. An economic gulf separates these from the vast farmer and laborer group, whose poverty makes them a genuine proletariat.

Until three generations ago the dominant Confucian ideology called for a static division of society into three classes. The highest of these was the samurai, who controlled the land, manned the learned professions, and administered the government; next came the peasantry, the main productive class, romantically adulated by their betters at the same time that they were kept in subservience to them; lowest were the townsmen, artisans and merchants. Society in the eighteenth and nineteenth centuries was actually more fluid than this. The growing wealth of certain members of the merchant class had already begun to give them prestige approaching that of the samurai. With the abolition of feudalism in the 1870's, samurai, to make a living, were forced into business, the professions, or the laboring class. A new ruling class took the place of the old feudal order and consisted of men of comparatively new wealth, with some of the more prosperous members of the old feudal and court nobility. Japanese society is still much less fluid than American, though new families have succeeded in making their way through to the aristocracy.

Another elite group in Japan is the official class. Sons of good families accept the inferior salaries of government positions for the sake of the prestige and security that membership in the bureaucracy traditionally entails. Even the policeman is looked up to by the public. Artists, scholars, and teachers too enjoy social prestige out of proportion to their economic position.

Feudal society included two pariah classes, the *eta* and the *hinin*. The former were a hereditary caste, performing several of the menial occupations that were taboo to orthodox Buddhists. Among these occupations were the slaughter of animals, the execution of criminals, and curiously, the manufacture and sale of footgear. The *hinin* were not a hereditary group but consisted of individuals who had lost caste by becoming beggars or criminals. Both classes were abolished as legal entities in the antifeudal decrees of early Meiji. Samurai, peasants, townsmen, and *eta* all alike became commoners. True social equality for the former *eta* has been much more difficult to achieve. Intermarriage with *eta* is still frowned upon by Japanese of other classes, and the ancient stigma still forces some of them into degrading occupations.

FAMILY ORGANIZATION

In Japan, as elsewhere, the family is the basic unit of society. Japanese law and custom, however, give the family greater authority over the lives of its members than in the West. American youths are legally free of parental authority at the age of twenty-one and in practice enjoy considerable independence of action years earlier. In Japan, on the other hand, men and women frequently depend for most of their adult lives on the judgments of their elders within the family. Japanese law defines as the fundamental kinship unit a household, domiciled together and normally headed by the eldest male within it. Household members include the wife of the family head, their eldest son and his family, and their other children, if unmarried. In custom, a Japanese woman belongs to her father's family until she is married and to that of her eldest son on the death of her husband. To ensure continuance of the male family line, couples without sons frequently resort to adoption. If there are daughters, a son-in-law may be adopted to inherit the family property and carry on the family name. Elders may in effect abdicate the parental authority while they are alive. In this case, the eldest son becomes the family head and his parents nominally are subsidiary members of the household. Households are legal institutions as well as social entities. Rationing to households rather than individuals and the registry of vital statistics and census figures in terms of families are present-day survivals of an age when the legal functions of a family were still more important. In feudal times households even shared legal responsibility for the crimes of individual members.

The position of women in the Japanese family has been gradually liberalized over a period of decades. They have long had the right to own property and to initiate divorce actions. With suffrage in 1946, they came to enjoy equal legal rights with men, though there can be no doubt that custom continues to place greater restrictions on their freedom than in most Western countries.

A typical instance of the operation of family authority is the manner in which marriages are contracted. The parents choose a mate for a marriageable son or daughter from among the children of families of their acquaintance. They do not arrange the marriage directly with the parents of the prospective spouse but employ a trusted friend of both the families to act as middleman. Only when the marriage arrangements have been decided upon by both the families do the young people meet each other to approve the match. By recent law parents may not force their children into marriage against their wishes. Even so, by the force of custom, most marriages are still by parental arrangement. As the social system permits relatively little comradeship between young men and women, love-matches cannot be depended on to provide spouses for all. Even when young people become engaged by their own choice, the actual marriage details are frequently arranged in the traditional way.

Members of a household are not equal in their privileges and responsibilities. Instead each has his rank in relation to each of the others, status as a rule increasing with age. Boys take the responsibility for the care and household training of their younger brothers and expect obedience from them in return. Sisters within a family have a similar set of relationships. The head of the household is usually the highest wage earner, if not the only one. His opinions count for much in vital family decisions on the marriage of the children, choice of a domicile, and the like. In addition, he enjoys highest prestige within the family, bathing first in the water the entire household shares and being served first at meals. His wife too has her areas of authority and responsibility. Since she spends most of the household's income, she naturally has the greatest freedom of decision as to how it is to be spent. Education of her children within the home is another of her provinces.

THE GREATER FAMILY

Kinship solidarity is by no means limited to the members of a single household. Members of one household, plus their aunts, uncles, and cousins to a fairly remote degree, comprise an extended family with important social functions. In a country with few facilities for the care of the aged, infirm, and indigent, security for these individuals is largely the responsibility of their relatives. If they have no immediate family on whom to rely, they must be taken care of by their more remote kin. (Farm communities and city neighborhoods frequently cooperate in similar fashion and assume group responsibility whenever individuals or families meet with ruinous calamities.) Related households cooperate closely in the management of property or businesses that they have inherited jointly.

Several instances survive from the days of hereditary trades, crafts, and occupations. In some highly specialized arts and crafts, a family apprenticeship system furnished the only practical means of training children from birth to carry on the family tradition. Actors in the traditional *kabuki* dramas, for example, are a guild of several interrelated families who maintain strict control over the casting of roles, the techniques of performances, and even the texts of the plays. Other such guilds are responsible for the continuance of traditions in painting, music, ceramics, and the like. In the inevitable cases in which families of artists or artisans fail to produce talented children to succeed them, they have recourse to the universally accepted custom of adoption.

The zaibatsu firms, which have supplied most of the capital, managed most of the trade and industry, and owned most of the wealth of modern Japan, are family corporations transmitting property in much the same way as in the family guilds. Some of these companies date from the early seventeenth century and have maintained strict inheritance of property and control until the very recent past. Venerable codes of house law prescribed relations of zaibatsu members within their families and with the outside world and, above all, guarded against the loss of control over the companies to outsiders. On the theory that Japan's concentration of wealth and industrial control was inimical to her development as a peaceful and democratic nation, the occupation forced zaibatsu companies to offer much of their stock for sale on the open exchange. The failure of this reform to effect any large-scale redistribution of economic control is evidence of the power of kinship solidarity in this important department of Japanese society.

EDUCATION

Before Meiji, schools were of two kinds: aristocratic academies for the inculcation of Confucian virtue and the study of the Chinese classics, and Buddhist temple-schools for the young of other social classes. Vocational education was from father to son, and women acquired whatever talents were thought essential to their cultivation at the hands of their mothers. The Meiji government early realized the necessity of a trained citizenry if Japan was to be brought up to the standards of Western countries. It set up elementary and secondary schools throughout the country under the close scrutiny of the Ministry of Education. Government-run universities and technical colleges were opened to students from a wide variety of social classes by a combination of low tuition and high admission standards. Girls had easy access to primary education, but higher education facilities for them were meager. From the start the government schools emphasized the training necessary to produce loyal citizens. The defect in the system was that too close control by the central government allowed reactionary leaders to ensure the perpetuation of reaction. Japanese education was undemocratic simply because Japan was not a democracy. Occupation reforms of the school system aimed to make it democratic by (1) increasing school facilities and thus permitting more students to go to school longer and (2) divorcing primary and secondary education from central control.

The system, as modified under the occupation, provides nine years' free, compulsory schooling in primary and lower secondary schools. At this level schools are coeducational. Admission to the three-year upper secondary course is by competitive examination. Tuition is charged and schools may or may not be coeducational. Vocational education starts on the upper secondary level and continues in specialized colleges or the technical departments of universities. Colleges and universities now have four-year courses, entered after twelve years of primary and secondary schooling, instead of the old three-year course, which one entered after fourteen years in the lower schools. Graduate schools in some colleges and universities are a recent innovation. There are nearly two hundred colleges and universities of all kinds, public and private, and these had a total enrollment in 1950 of more than 500,000.

The elementary curriculum regularly includes Japanese reading and writing, arithmetic, social studies, science, music, drawing, handicrafts, and physical education. The teaching of reading and writing predominates, for Japanese writing is an even greater academic time-consumer than English spelling. A postwar reform abolished the teaching of military training and of *shūshin,* or "ethics," the latter because it included the inculcation of militaristic and chauvinistic ideals inconsistent with the occupation's program of democratization. Textbooks in all courses have been revised to rid them of supernationalistic flavor.

Standards of university scholarship are high, in accordance

with the best Western traditions, German, English, and American. The introduction of coeducation in the national universities after the war offers women for the first time what the Japanese consider to be their highest quality of advanced instruction.

The proportion of employed Japanese in various types of occupations in 1950, as compared with 1940, is as follows:

	PERCENTAGE EMPLOYED	
	1950	*1940*
Agriculture and Fishing	48.5	44.1
Mining	1.5	1.8
Construction	4.0	3.0
Manufacturing	15.8	21.2
Commerce and Finance	11.8	13.6
Transportation and Communications	5.0	4.7
Professions	9.0	9.0
Government Service	4.1	1.9
Unclassified	0.3	0.7

Japanese folk toys attest to the ingenuity of the Japanese in using simple ideas and economical materials. Some are objects of true folk art, associated with local craft traditions. Native games, too, utilize simple basic ideas, though the two most famous of them, *shôgi,* or "Japanese chess," and *gô,* are games of skill demanding intelligence and much practice for their mastery.

Traditional recreations for the masses center in the holidays and festival seasons. Some of these are of purely political or national significance and include the birthday of the present Emperor (April 29), Constitution Day (commemorating the enforcement of the new Constitution on May 3, 1947), and Culture Day (November 3, dedicated to the promotion of culture as a concern of a peace-loving people). Celebrations at the vernal and autumnal equinoxes are Shinto festivals. The former is traditionally the time for nation-wide veneration of ancestors. Thanksgiving Day (November 23) perpetuates the old Shinto ceremonies of dedication of crops. Children's Day (May 5) is a national holiday on the date of the old Boys' Festival, featuring kite-flying competitions. Girls' Day (March 3) is a time for displaying dolls. Most important of the holiday seasons is the New Year, which lasts most of the month of January. Religious and secular observances associated with this season include formal calls on business and social acquaintances, family visits to neighborhood shrines, games of battledore and shuttlecock, and the consumption of much *mochi,* the hard, glutinous rice-cakes reserved for this time of year.

Flower arranging, the tea ceremony, gardening (on a very small scale), the chanting of *yôkyoku* (texts of the classical *nô* dramas), photography, and calligraphy are among the minor arts cultivated by many Japanese as hobbies.

Traditional sports were encouraged before the war as aids to the cultivation of military spirit and self-control. Most famous of these were *jûdô* and *kendô,* or fencing. *Sumô,* the major native spectator sport, is a highly stylized form of wrestling practiced by giants purposely trained and overfed from infancy by the family guilds to which they belong. Western sports are universally popular. Baseball, both of the sand-lot variety played by practically all boys and as a spectator sport by college teams, is the national game. The physical characteristics of the Japanese especially suit them to sports of speed and agility such as tennis and swimming.

WAY OF LIFE AND LIVING STANDARD

Evaluation of Japan's living standard depends on the norm one wishes to apply. Though restricted in comparison to some European and American countries, Japan comes closer to providing the essentials for comfort than most other countries of the Far East. Ignoring for a moment the very real deficiency in diet available to the average Japanese, it can be said that the relatively simple and economical way of life allows people of modest means to satisfy most of their basic demands. The living conditions of the average family illustrate the means by which material limitations have been minimized. Families are large and houses small; hence privacy within the household is nonexistent. Yet a fenced enclosure containing house and yard offers each family its aloofness and individuality. Except in city slums, each has its miniature garden. Long-standing customs eliminate the need for elaborate furnishings, for Japanese do not find it uncomfortable to sit or sleep on their floor mats of padded straw. Removal of shoes in houses keeps floors clean enough to make this possible. The Japanese bathe often—daily, if water and fuel permit—at home or, for those too poor to have the facilities in their houses, in inexpensive public baths. Lest the close-knit, authoritarian families appear unbearably austere, it should be stressed that they are built on affection, particularly for children, to as great an extent as in any society. The fond parent, overindulgent toward his small children, is as typical in fact as in folklore. Sternness toward one's children comes only at the age in their lives when they may be expected to shoulder the responsibilities of adulthood. As for the possibilities of genuine affection between husbands and wives who started their married life as complete strangers to one another, one can only point out that unhappy marriages seem no commoner than under any other system.

To the limit of their economic circumstances, the Japanese love to travel. Family cars are next to nonexistent and roads unsuited to automobile travel, but railroads go within a few miles of almost every point in Japan and offer the people one of their characteristic diversions. Sightseeing in historic or scenic places, mountain-climbing, and skiing are popular enough to make tourism more than just a major "export industry." It is a domestic industry as well.

A word on health and sanitation: overcrowding, diet deficiencies, and inadequate sanitary facilities make for a serious public health problem requiring all the resources of Japan's advanced medical science to keep under control. The incidence of tuberculosis is high, while heroic efforts have been required on a few occasions since the war to prevent typhus and smallpox outbreaks from reaching serious epidemic proportions. Diseases of sanitation are common, owing partly to the use of night soil as fertilizer. For reasons of economy, sudden substitution of a safer sewage disposal system would create more serious problems than it would solve. On the brighter side, standards of medical techniques and equipment are high, and the relatively new science of public health continues to make progress in improving the nation's health. Noticeable reduction since the war of the death rate from tuberculosis is only one of several comparable accomplishments.

Linguists assign Japanese to a language family by itself. Only one other language is obviously related to it, the language of the Ryukyu Islands; and that is so closely related that it may be considered a dialect of Japanese. Hence there is no really convincing evidence as to the origins of the language. Many attempts have been made to relate Japanese to the language families of Asia as well as to the Malayo-Polynesian languages. Similarities of structure to these languages seem more than accidental, but students still hesitate to consider them conclusive evidence of language kinship. The Chinese language is completely unlike Japanese in structure and native vocabulary, though modern Japanese has thousands of words borrowed from Chinese just as modern English has countless words of Latin or Greek derivation. The common misapprehension that Japanese is similar linguistically to Chinese is explained by the accident that Japanese is written with Chinese characters.

Chinese loan words in Japanese include many signifying things or concepts unknown to the primitive Japanese people. Some, such as *fude,* "writing brush," and *uma,* "horse," became fully naturalized Japanese words at a very early date, while others, such as *bôzu,* "Buddhist priest," and *seiji,* "government," represent borrowing at a more advanced state of Japanese civilization. An interesting class of Chinese derivatives in modern Japanese contains words coined in Japan to meet the demands of modern science and technology. Examples are *jidôsha,* "automobile," from three Chinese elements meaning self-moving vehicle, and *genshi,* "atom," meaning, more or less, "original thing."

The Japanese have adapted the Chinese characters to their own language in an ingenious, but unwieldy, way. Japanese words with close equivalents in Chinese—most nouns, verbs, and adjectives—are written with the appropriate Chinese characters. Particles and other grammatical devices having no exact equivalents in Chinese are represented phonetically with symbols called *kana,* which the Japanese themselves invented by modifying certain of the Chinese ideographs. Each of the forty-eight *kana* represents a syllable, and one could, if one wished, write Japanese exclusively by means of them. Marked benefits seem possible from such a system, for *kana* orthography exhibits none of the vagaries of English, or even French, spelling. The possible benefits of adopting a phonetic system, either *kana* or the Roman alphabet, seem so obvious, in fact, that non-Japanese frequently ask just why it has never been tried. At such a question there ensues a passionate argument on the language reform issue, the Japanese siding almost unanimously, but almost alone, against reform. The reformers point out the following advantages to be gained:

1. The long hours Japanese school children spend learning to read and write their own language could be better spent at content courses in the natural and social sciences or the humanities.

2. The mechanics of printing and typing would be greatly simplified.

3. A common system of writing with Western countries

would facilitate Japanese study of Western languages and hence Western culture.

4. Japanese technical and scientific writings, now all but unknown to Western scholars, would be more readily available to them.

In answer, the Japanese point out that:

1. A switch to a new system would within a generation make the classics of their own literature unavailable to them.

2. It would block them off from the civilization of China.

3. It would necessitate troublesome modification of their own language, for the diversity of the Chinese characters allows a larger vocabulary in written Japanese than the overly simple sound system permits in speech.

4. It would be an unnecessary inconvenience for a country already 99-plus percent literate to change anything so habitual as a writing system.

INTELLECTUAL LIFE

Japan's publishing industry is one of the world's largest and most vigorous. The Japanese as a whole are great readers and, as a consequence, a wide range of reading material is available to the public at remarkably low prices. Public libraries are comparatively new in Japan and as yet satisfy only a tiny fraction of the demand for popular books.

There is no limit to the range of subjects about which Japanese read. It is to be expected that American and European affairs, manners, customs, and civilization have been consuming interests in all classes of Japanese society since the advent of westernization nearly a century ago. Books on all phases of their own national life are equally popular.

Middle and higher schools stress the study of literature, and their graduates are as a rule well read in the classics of East and West. The novels of nineteenth-century Russia and of twentieth-century France are especially popular, though there has been an increase in interest in English and American fiction since the war. Translations of literature from all the major European languages exist in great number; some popular works have been translated many times. Japan has only recently become a signatory to the International Copyright Agreement, so that most of the existing translations, even those from living authors, were produced at lower costs than in the case of native books.

Japanese literature makes use of all the native conventions and traditions, though it has been influenced to a considerable degree by European literature. The average quality is perhaps no higher than anywhere else. Magazines cater to a wide range of interest—scholarly, technical, popular, and political.

Two or three of the Tokyo and Osaka dailies have circulations among the highest of any newspapers in the world. The severe postwar shortage of newsprint has not entirely abated, with the result that even the largest metropolitan papers are limited to six to eight pages per issue. The range of coverage in the dailies of national circulation is substantially the same as in America, news of national and international significance all but crowding out stories of purely local interest to the cities in which they are published. In addition, there are many feature stories, columns on homemaking, entertainment, fine arts, and finance, and editorials. A large number of provincial papers specialize in local news. In 1950 the 190 dailies in Japan had a combined circulation of 20,400,000; 340 non-daily papers had a circulation of 6,920,000.

Japanese scientists compete on terms of equality with those of the rest of the world and many have been noteworthy contributors to world scientific knowledge at the highest level. There have been outstanding contributors in all the branches of physical and biological science as well as mathematics. The list includes, among many others, the chemist Takamine Jôkichi, who first synthesized adrenalin in 1901; Noguchi Hideyo, a doctor who made important contributions to the pathology of yellow fever and syphilis; and the Nobel Prize-winning physicist, Yukawa Hideki, whose prediction of the meson paved the way for later experimental confirmation.

READINGS

Benedict, Ruth. *The Chrysanthemum and the Sword; Patterns of Japanese Culture.* Boston, Houghton Mifflin, 1946.

Ishimoto, Shidzue. *Facing Two Ways; the Story of My Life.* New York, Farrar and Rinehart, 1935.

Sugimoto, Etsu. *A Daughter of the Samurai.* Garden City, Doubleday, Page, 1925.

Vining, Elizabeth Gray. *Windows for the Crown Prince.* Philadelphia, Lippincott, 1952.

FILMS

The Japanese Family. International Film Foundation, Inc., 345 East 46th Street, New York 17, N.Y.

Kimono. Japan Travel Information Office, 10 Rockefeller Plaza, New York 20, N.Y.

Tooru's People. Religious Film Association, 45 Astor Place, New York 3, N.Y.

FINE ARTS

The main line of the Japanese artistic tradition dates from shortly after the introduction of Buddhism from the Continent in the sixth century of the Christian era. All the major fine arts in Japan—painting, sculpture, and architecture—took their first inspirations from the traditions, already refined and sophisticated when they reached Japan, of India, China, and Korea. Art of succeeding periods continued to be influenced by new developments on the mainland, though Japan's increased isolation from the rest of the Far East from the ninth to the fourteenth centuries encouraged her artists to apply their own native genius to the borrowed tradition. The most vigorous Japanese art of the past three or four centuries is obviously related to the art of China, but much that is most characteristic about it is wholly Japanese.

Buddhism has played much the same role in the development of Japanese art that Christianity has in the European artistic tradition. For a long while most of the art patronage and much of the actual skill and knowledge in artistic techniques were provided by the Buddhist monasteries in Japan or by missionary priests from abroad. As a result, the subject matter of Japanese art in this period was predominantly religious—aspects of the

Buddha or incidents of his life, Buddhist divinities and holy men, and scenes from the religious life of the people. Even when at a later date Japanese painters began to specialize in landscapes, portraiture, and other kinds of secular art, many of them were priests who depended on monastic institutions for their training and livelihood. Even the secular works of such artists frequently illustrate in subtle fashion Buddhist ways of thought.

Buddhist art and the classical art in imitation of Chinese styles both reflected the tastes of the Japanese upper classes. Parallel to this sort of aristocratic art, there existed a tradition of folk arts and crafts predominantly secular and designed for the appreciation of the middle classes. The woodblock prints of the seventeenth, eighteenth, and nineteenth centuries were works of this kind, produced in great quantity and reckoned of no lasting value; yet they were works of skilled craftsmanship and artistic sophistication. Similarly, minor arts such as textiles and ceramics displayed technical virtuosity and aesthetic taste, even when designed for the enjoyment of humble folk.

ANCIENT ART (TO CA. 600 A.D.)

Pre-Buddhist art in Japan is of more than purely archaeological interest, though the techniques were primitive and the range of subject matter narrow. Copper and bronze utensils indicate early (*ca.* first century) knowledge from the Asiatic continent of casting techniques.

Ancient artifacts have been found chiefly in or near the burial mounds of the period, indicating a ritual significance for these works. (If nonritual art objects existed, they have not been preserved.) Finds include tools and weapons of stone and metal, pottery, jewels, and rude clay figures of men and animals, known as *haniwa*.

More or less intelligent guesses as to the nature of the earliest architecture have been made from non-Chinese elements in traditional Japanese houses and from ancient temple buildings of distinctive style that have been repaired and rebuilt continually since unrecorded antiquity. Ancient buildings were probably of wood or bamboo construction with rain-resistant reed or bark roofs and raised floors.

ART OF THE EARLY BUDDHIST PERIOD (TO CA. 800)

Many splendid examples of Buddhist sculpture of this period have been preserved in temples and monasteries. Those of the sixth and seventh centuries are of wood or bronze, whereas eighth-century pieces include some of clay or dry lacquer. There is no suitable stone, either for sculpture or as building material, in Japan. Statues are stylized and symbolic rather than literally representational, though the best examples give no feeling of naïveté or of clumsy technique. Pieces range in scale from devotional images a few inches high to the 53-foot bronze Buddha in the Tôdai-ji in Nara.

Such architecture as remains from the period consists largely in temple buildings of Chinese style. The main hall (Kon-dô) and pagoda of the Hôryû-ji near Nara are the oldest wooden buildings in the world. They are of special interest to students of oriental architecture, since constant repairing has splendidly preserved them as specimens of the Chinese wooden temple construction no longer extant on the Continent.

Painting was an adjunct to religious architecture. The best

extant pieces are the suavely stylized panel scenes on the
Tamamushi-zushi, a small shrine in the Hôryû-ji, and the
murals of divinities and bodhisattvas in the main hall of the
same temple. (The last-named paintings, well preserved for
twelve centuries, were extensively damaged by fire in 1949.)

The minor arts such as metalwork, textiles, musical instruments, and ceramics were appreciated in Japan of the Nara
period. The collection now preserved in the Shôsô-in Imperial
Treasury in Nara are unrivaled examples of the craftsmanship
of the eighth-century civilizations of China and even Persia.
Many of the pieces were undoubtedly imported to Japan, though
many others were of Japanese manufacture.

HEIAN ART (800–1200)

The removal of the capital to Kyoto in 794 marked only a
minor break in the artistic tradition. Buddhism remained the
major Japanese religion, and the fine arts continued to be patronized by the clergy or by pious laymen. A more important
influence on Japanese art was the gradual cessation of direct
official relations with China. The political power of the cul-
turally brilliant T'ang dynasty in China was in dissolution after
the late eighth century. The dynasty fell in 906. The last of
many embassies to China of Japanese priests, officials, and
artists was in 838. Thereafter, for more than five hundred years,
the only intercourse between the two countries was occasional
unofficial visits by priests or traders. Japan was never in complete isolation from the artistic influence of the Continent, but
Japanese artists did cultivate greater originality during this
period than before. Sculpture of the Heian period is similar

in forms and content to the earlier pieces, though it is much inferior in vigor.

Architecture also suffered for a time from the cessation of fresh stimulation from China. One of the few remaining master-works from the period is the Phoenix Hall (Hôô-dô) of the Byôdô-in at Uji, a temple dating from 1056. The attenuated symmetry of the roof lines suggests to some the delicate balance of a poised bird and is a mark of a more native Japanese taste.

The Heian period produced the first paintings of a new and completely Japanese manner known as *Yamato-e*. These scrolls and painted fans and ornaments are secular in feeling, take their subject matter from the everyday life of people of all classes, and exhibit great animation and grace of composition. Many of the Buddhist paintings of the Heian period are master-pieces of world rank.

KAMAKURA ART (1200–1400)

Social and religious changes that accompanied the advent of feudal government at Kamakura in the late twelfth century altered the role of the arts in contemporary life. The new aris-tocracy were no longer effete courtiers but military men of simple, vigorous tastes. The flourishing Buddhist sects of the period were less philosophically abstruse and of greater appeal to the common people, and reflected in their artistic canons the same simplicity and directness that characterized their tenets of belief.

In the thirteenth century, Japanese sculpture achieved its last and greatest virtuosity. Unkei (twelfth to thirteenth century) and his school produced wooden religious images and portrait statues ranging in expression from the greatest violence to the most serene spirituality. Anatomical faithfulness to nature gives these works an appearance of "realism" in contrast to the frank stylizations of earlier sculpture.

The giant bronze Buddha (Daibutsu) at Kamakura dates from 1252. Even so technically unwieldy a form as this exemplifies the expressiveness that Kamakura sculptors mastered.

The earliest Japanese Zen monasteries date from the thirteenth century and are of a newly imported, unostentatious style in keeping with the tenets of the sect. Dwellings of the feudal aristocracy were fortresses and, like the Zen temples, were of tasteful simplicity.

Kamakura painting is distinguished for the variety of its themes and the vigor and realism with which they are portrayed. Religious scenes skillfully use fire, cloud, and landscape background not as mere ornament but to heighten the emotional qualities of the composition. Landscapes of familiar Japanese places were early instances of the imparting of spiritual qualities to wholly secular subject matter. Priests, legendary Buddhist patriarchs, and even supernatural beings emerge from the religious art of the period as individuals, and the portraits of contemporary personages (such as that of Minamoto Yoritomo, who founded the Kamakura shogunate) are masterpieces of personality suggestion. Most impressive of all the Kamakura paintings perhaps are the scrolls (*emaki-mono*) illustrating many kinds of religious and secular narrative. Their styles are as varied as the subjects represented. Most of them are further developments of the *Yamato-e* style.

MUROMACHI ART (1400–1568)

The political disunity that prevailed under the later Ashikaga shoguns was no deterrent to the brilliance of the arts they patronized. Indeed, shoguns like Ashikaga Yoshimasa (reigned 1449–74) seem to have allowed their love of elegance and luxury to divert attention from the really pressing problems of the time, those of endemic warfare and political dissolution. Rulers of the Ashikaga family built the period's two most noteworthy architectural monuments, the Golden Pavilion (Kinkaku-ji, destroyed by fire in 1950) and the Silver Pavilion (Ginkaku-ji), as residences. The former dated from 1397, was of unostentatious taste except for the gilt of its interior apartments, and merged with complete success into its garden setting. The Silver Pavilion, which still stands, achieved elegance through an even greater restraint approaching plainness.

The artistic canons of the Zen sect were a healthful influence on painting in the Muromachi period, for at the same time that they encouraged the strictest economy in the use of line and color, they freed the talents of Zen painters for the widest variety of themes. Formal devotional images and scenes from the supernatural never again found much favor among either artists or patrons of art. They gave way to landscapes, nature studies, and scenes from secular life. Japanese artists of the Muromachi period carried on a great Chinese painting tradition that dated from the Sung dynasty (tenth to thirteenth centuries). Josetsu and Shûbun were early fifteenth-century masters of the Japanese ink-painting style that culminated a hundred years later in the work of Sesshû (1420–1506) and his school. The Kano school, a more native adaptation of the Sung landscape tradition, stemmed from the work of two Muromachi painters, Kano Masanobu (1453–90) and Kano Motonobu (1476–1559).

MOMOYAMA ART (1568–1615)

Momoyama is an area in the southern environs of Kyoto where Toyotomi Hideyoshi erected a fortress-palace in 1594. The architectural monuments of the period to which it gave its name were lavishly decorated and of impressive scale, reflecting not only the wealth of their builders, of whom the low-born Hide-yoshi was typical, but also their standards of taste, untutored and unrefined in comparison with those of the Muromachi aristocrats. The sixteenth-century introduction to Japan of West-ern firearms necessitated a type of fortress similar in construc-tion to contemporary European castles. Japanese architects com-bined the European principles of defense with characteristically oriental features of design to produce the many castles of the period. The castle at Himeji (1581) is a well-preserved example of this unique form. The gigantic keep of the Osaka castle was rebuilt in 1931, but it is faithful in external details to Hideyoshi's original fortress on the same site. Specimens of walls, moats, and out-buildings from castles no longer intact may be seen in the Imperial Palace in Tokyo and at the site of the Nagoya castle.

Gardens too were of unprecedented magnificence. The Japa-nese art of landscape gardening was never used to create formally patterned gardens of the European fashion but instead aimed as far as possible at the reproduction of natural landscape beauty, often at prodigious expense of labor and materials.

Momoyama painting was opulent and ostentatious. Wholly

secularized under the patronage of the great military rulers, it abandoned the economy and subtlety of the Muromachi schools, preserving their exquisite craftsmanship and sense of design. Dazzlingly colorful screen-paintings of flowers, birds, and landscapes were commissioned by the score as ornaments for Momoyama palaces.

Japanese ceramic art had been encouraged by the vogue for the tea ceremony that started in the fifteenth century. The semi-ritual nature of the ceremony as originally practiced by devotees of Zen called for extreme austerity of design in the bowls and utensils used. An art was made of achieving the proper degree of roughness and gracelessness, with the paradoxical result that some of the least prepossessing of the Muromachi art objects (to the untrained eye) soon came to be esteemed as priceless masterworks. The spirit of the Momoyama period, however, disdained economy and called for show. The ornate and colorful bowls and dishes typical of that time opened the way for a great variety of graceful and useful ceramic objects in the following period.

TOKUGAWA ART (1615–1868)

The age of the Tokugawa shoguns was one of peace, of gradual decrease in the vitality of the Buddhist sects, and of the growth of cities and a prosperous merchant class. While the art of the classic schools tended to decline still further in originality and strength, popular arts and folkcrafts flourished as never before with the patronage of city-dwelling samurai and merchants.

While Buddhist architecture fell into repetitions of old styles and increasingly elaborate products of Momoyama decorativeness (for example, the gorgeously carved and painted but overly fussy temples at Nikkô), one branch of architecture reached new heights of formal clarity and functional efficiency. This was domestic architecture, a hybrid development from native and Chinese elements.

Schools of painting proliferated in the seventeenth century. The Kano school broke up into several traditions, each with its unique qualities; the decorative art of the Momoyama period influenced several major Tokugawa artists, of whom Kôrin (1658–1716) is best known; the *Yamato-e* tradition produced an important new school, the Sumiyoshi, that was to be a forerunner of the woodblock print schools of the eighteenth and nineteenth centuries. Western painting was known to the Japanese as early as the mid-sixteenth century and in the seventeenth inspired a minor school in partial imitation of it, specializing in scenes of Japanese commerce with westerners. Maruyama Ôkyo (1733–95) introduced a new realism in his studies of birds and animals and established a school influenced to some extent by Western illustration.

Most celebrated of the Tokugawa arts is that of *ukiyo-e,* the paintings and block prints designed for mass distribution to city dwellers of all social classes. In the latter part of the seventeenth century print artists such as Hishikawa Moronobu (d. ca. 1694) and Torii Kiyonobu (1664–1729) began to manufacture pictures of actors, a type of *ukiyo-e* that was to become one of the most characteristic. The early prints were in black and white but were sometimes hand-colored. Color printing was invented about 1741 and full-color printing about 1765. More sophisticated use of the block-cutting techniques and greater freedom of design and subject matter in the latter part of the eighteenth century led the art to its culmination under such masters as Harunobu (1724–70), Utamaro (1754–1806), and Sharaku (painted 1794–95). The last named specialized entirely in theatrical prints and was a master caricaturist. Hokusai (1760–1849) and Hiroshige (1797–1858) were artists of originality and integrity in an age when the art as a whole had begun to decline.

Brief mention should be made of the countless objects of everyday use that became works of art at the hands of Tokugawa craftsmen: pottery, brass or iron utensils, folk-toys, fans, lacquer trays, boxes and tobacco pouches, *netsuke* (carved wood or ivory pendants), and the like.

MODERN ART (SINCE 1868)

The masters of the *ukiyo-e* created Japan's last great art of a distinctive and indigenous style. There have been many innovations in the hundred years or so since the death of Hokusai and Hiroshige, and they have literally revolutionized the fine arts, but all these innovations have been of Western, not Eastern, origin. The process of westernization began late in the Tokugawa period in the prints and paintings of artistic radicals like Shiba Kôkan (1747–1818) and Watanabe Kazan (1793–1841), both of whom experimented with scientific laws of perspective and other approaches to realism. The craze for westernization during the Meiji period (1868–1912) brought to the attention of the Japanese all the achievements of Western art, allowing them to go the limit in slavish imitation of a myriad of its varieties. The result was often an affront to the taste of both civilizations, but in the long run such a mingling of traditions produced much fine work by Japanese artists. A contrary process by which Western artists in the latter part of the nineteenth century discovered the values of Japanese painting and decorative arts brought the traditions of the two cultures still closer together, eventuating in a contemporary art in Japan that is not so much Western as international.

READINGS

Fenollosa, Ernest Francisco. *Epochs of Chinese and Japanese Art; an Outline History of Asiatic Design.* New and rev. ed. with copious notes by Professor Petrucci, 2 vols. New York, Stokes, 1921.

Henderson, H. G., and R. T. Paine, Jr. *The University Prints. Series O, Section III. Japanese Art.* Newton, Mass., The University Prints, 1939.

Minamoto, H. *An Illustrated History of Japanese Art.* Translated by Harold G. Henderson. Kyoto, Hoshino, 1935.

Tsuda, Noritake. *Handbook of Japanese Art.* Tokyo, Sanseidô, 1935.

Warner, Langdon. *The Enduring Art of Japan.* Cambridge, Harvard University Press, 1952.

FILMS

Advancing Kyoto. Japan Travel Information Office, 10 Rockefeller Plaza, New York 20, N.Y.

Ancient Sculpture of Japan. Japan Travel Information Office, 10 Rockefeller Plaza, New York 20, N.Y.

Ceramics of Japan. Information Section of the Embassy of Japan, 2514 Massachusetts Ave., N.W., Washington 8, D.C.

Conspiracy in Kyoto. Indiana University, Division of Adult Education and Public Services, Audio-Visual Center, Bloomington, Indiana.

LITERATURE

The poetry and prose of Japan have throughout history been under a certain debt to the literature of China. Several features, however, have been wholly Japanese. For example, the novel had an independent development in Japan, actually maturing earlier there than it did in China; indigenous elements in the Japanese drama created two unique forms of theater, the *nô* and the *kabuki;* in addition, differences between the Chinese and Japanese languages made for wide variance between the poetic forms of the two countries. Modern Japan has borrowed heavily from the forms, themes, and techniques of Western literature, though certain native traits have retained their popularity with contemporary writers. In particular, Japanese poetry of traditional style and a characteristic type of informal essay, called *zuihitsu,* continue to occupy important places in the contemporary literary scene.

Terseness is a frequently cited characteristic of Japanese literature; long poems are rare, though long prose works are, with some notable exceptions, collections of more or less independent fragments or episodes. Many Western commentators have noted that the emotional range of Japanese poetry and prose fiction is comparatively limited; repressed love, sorrows of

parting, world-weariness, and the apprehension of earthly eva-
nescence loom large among their themes. Japanese writers often
framed these sentiments in language of the greatest subtlety
and delicacy but rarely transcended them into the realms more
esteemed in Western writing of personalized passion or trag-
edy. Yet the finest Japanese literature succeeds in being spirited
and moving to the very degree that the casualness and indirec-
tion of its expression suggest the writer's convictions about the
universal human issues of aspiration, contention, resignation,
love, and death.

EARLY POETRY

The primitive Japanese language had no alphabet; the earliest
literature consisted in rituals and chronicles preserved for an
indeterminate number of years in an oral tradition before
finally being written down about the seventh or eighth century.

A few secular verses from ancient times have been incorporated into the earliest chronicles. A far more important collection of early poetry, however, is the *Man'yô-shû* (Collection of a
Myriad Leaves) compiled toward the close of the Nara period.
There are more than four thousand poems in the collection,
most of them dating from the seventh and eighth centuries.
The *Man'yô-shû* was compiled under the auspices of the
Imperial Court and reflects the outlook of the aristocracy of the
time. A few songs of the nature of folk poetry deal with peasant
life; other poems make reference to the life of border guards
stationed in the distant eastern provinces. These help round out
the picture the collection gives of the social life of the age. The
poems are mostly short, occasional lyrics of fresh, sensuous lan-

guage. Rhyme has no place in Japanese poetry. Instead, the *Man'yô-shû*—in common with most later poetry—makes use of patterns of line length to provide formal regularity. The most common pattern alternates five-syllable and seven-syllable lines, finishing with an additional line of seven syllables, thus: 5, 7, 5, 7 . . . 5, 7, 7. The classic form is the *tanka,* or brief poem, of five lines in the pattern 5, 7, 5, 7, 7.

There were many later collections of verse of the general style of the *Man'yô-shû,* the most famous being the *Kokin-shû* (Collection of Poems, Ancient and Modern), of the early tenth century, and *Shin-kokin-shû,* of the early thirteenth.

CLASSIC PROSE

Native Japanese prose was in some respects an outgrowth of poetry. The earliest prose masterwork in Japanese is the preface to the *Kokin-shû,* written by its compiler, Ki-no-Tsurayuki (883–946), and dealing with the nature of poetry. Early works of fiction consisted of narratives interspersed with verses that expressed in terse form the emotional flavor of the story. There is some reason to believe that such collections were thought of primarily as anthologies of poems and that the narratives that fill them out were meant to be explanations of the verse parts. Leaving aside the primitive legends and other narratives that are to be found in the early chronicles, the principal milestones of the development of Japanese fiction are the *Taketori Mono-gatari* (The Bamboo-cutter's Tale), an extended fairy tale of the ninth century, the *Ise Monogatari* (Tales of Ise), of the tenth, and the *Yamato Monogatari* (Tales of Yamato), of the eleventh.

Supplementing supernatural and poetical fiction were other prose works of an informal nature: travel diaries and notebooks of brief anecdotes and impressions. Such forms were considered appropriate to the Japanese language, whereas more ponderous works of the same age were customarily written in Chinese, the prestige language. The impressive number of women who contributed to the development of Japanese prose stems from the curious feature in the social structure that made Chinese the language of government, religion, and classical learning—in short, the literary language for men. Ki-no-Tsurayuki freely admitted that in writing the *Kokin-shû* preface and the *Tosa Nikki* (best known of the Heian travel diaries), he was adopting the "women's language," that is to say, Japanese. The best of the literary notebooks is the *Makura no Sôshi* (Pillow Book) of Sei Shônagon, a court lady who wrote about 1000 A.D. It is filled with perceptive, elegantly phrased comments on art, human nature, and the workings of court society.

The *Genji Monogatari* (Tale of Genji) by Murasaki Shikibu, another court lady and a contemporary of Sei Shônagon, is a narrative of the refined court life with which Lady Murasaki was familiar. Like earlier fictional works it abounds in verses dashed off by its characters in moments of emotional stress in lieu of the inelegant bluntness of prose speech. Unlike all previous Japanese works, it unfolds a single sustained story in which the characters behave from motivations of lifelike complexity. It is, in fact, the first true Japanese novel and has been called, moreover, the world's first great work of prose fiction. It is ostensibly a biography of a brilliant sensualist, Prince Genji, whose lifetime of amatory adventures amid surroundings of luxury and refinement aptly illustrates the themes

dominant in Japanese literature of the illusoriness of pleasure
and the transience of the material world.

The Japanese learned their historiography from China and
contributed little that was new to it. Early in the Nara period
(eighth century) the Court ordered the ancient legends and
chronicles of Japan to be compiled and set down in Japanese.
These were the *Kojiki,* or "Chronicles of Ancient Events." Six
official histories in the Chinese language documented the history
of the Imperial Court down to about 900. These were the so-
called six national histories, all of them of an unadorned chronological style. History became an important branch of literature
later in the Heian period with a number of works of colorful
narrative style. Some of these, like the *Ô-Kagami* (a biography
of the eleventh-century regent Fujiwara Michinaga), were
chronicles of court life; others, like the *Heike Monogatari*
(Tales of the Heike), which dealt with the interclan wars of
the twelfth century, were primarily battle accounts. Historians
of the feudal Middle Ages (thirteenth to sixteenth centuries)
combined the narrative interest of these chronicles with political
or moral purpose. Kitabatake Chikafusa (1293–1354) typified
this sort of history in the *Jinnô-shôtô-ki* (Chronicle of the True
Dynasty), written during the dynastic schism of the fourteenth
century; Chikafusa aimed to prove the justice of the southern
dynasty's claims to legitimacy. The Tokugawa era produced a
number of histories based on formal Chinese models. One of
them, the *Honchô Tsugan,* compiled by the official academy
of the shogun's court, was a strictly chronological general

history of Japan. Another, the *Dai-Nihon-shi,* or "History of Japan," was arranged topically in the manner of the official dynastic histories of China. It was written by scholars at the court of the fief of Mito and supported the notion, familiar to students of recent Japanese history, of the sacred character of the Imperial dynasty.

THE NÔ DRAMA

Japanese classic drama grew out of Shinto or Buddhist ritual dance-plays of Nara and Heian times. In the fourteenth century a group of entertainers with the patronage of the Ashikaga shoguns brought together elements from the old theater and refined them into a highly stylized dramatic form known as *nô*. It is drama of the greatest austerity, understatement being its dominating feature in text, staging, and performance. The brief poetic plays usually underline a Buddhist or, more rarely, Shinto moral and often feature supernatural events and characters. Often the events that constitute the drama are not acted on the stage at all but are described by their protagonists as having taken place years earlier. Actors eke out the extremely limited range of bodily gesture permitted by the classic canons with dances suggestive of the feeling of the drama while choruses reminiscent of those in Greek drama relate or amplify the action from the side of the stage. The performance of these plays is of too recondite a character to have retained a great modern following even among Japanese, though the texts are still greatly appreciated in Japan for their moral loftiness and poetic beauty.

TOKUGAWA THEATER

The urban and middle-class culture of the seventeenth and eighteenth centuries brought forth new dramatic forms of far greater popular appeal than the aristocratic *nô* dramas. The most important of these from the literary point of view was the *jôruri* theater, in which the action was carried out as realistically as possible on a stage by puppets about half life-size and the dialogue and choric commentary intoned from the side by a single performer known as the *jôruri*. The plays themselves were often adaptations of *nô* dramas, but the language was modernized and colloquial, and the performance, save that it was by dolls rather than people, was more realistic in every respect. The best-known dramatist was Chikamatsu Monzae-mon (1653–1725).

The *kabuki* drama was a further step in the direction of theatrical realism. Performed by live actors on huge stages, usually with elaborate scenery and brilliant costumes, it nevertheless retains some of the stylizations of its predecessors, *nô* and the doll-dramas. Some of the artificialities of performance, in fact, are conscious imitations of the halting, awkward movements of puppets. The plays are often mere adaptations of those used in the puppet theater, but elaboration by generations of actors has made the best known of them much longer than the seventeenth-century originals. Single plays lasting the better part of a day are not unusual. The artistic distinction of the *kabuki* theater lies not in the literary qualities of the plays but in the brilliance of the acting tradition. As hybrid productions of dialogue, music, and the dance, they can be quite effective theater, and it is this fact that has preserved the *kabuki* as the only truly living branch of Japan's classic theatrical art.

HAIKU AND SENRYÛ

The *tanka* verse form lost popularity in the seventeenth century to another still briefer and more indirect type of expression. This was the *haiku*, a three-line form of seventeen syllables in the arrangement 5, 7, 5. By convention *haiku* were associated with seasons of the year, and their writers sought in them to evoke striking impressions of the qualities of nature with the greatest economy of words. So brief a form could hardly bring forth more than mere suggestions of poetic ideas, somewhat as though single lines from European lyric poetry were made to stand alone as complete poems. Even today practically all literate Japanese try their hand at the form at some time or other, though the greatest *haiku* poets were of the school of Bashô (1644–94).

Senryû were of the same length and syllabic arrangements as *haiku* but were humorous, satiric, or epigrammatic.

THE TOKUGAWA NOVEL

A revival of fiction during the Tokugawa period stemmed, as had the contemporary developments in the theater, from the diffusion of literate culture to members of the new townsman class. As in the case of the classic productions of the Heian period, short stories and novels played delicately or indelicately with themes of unrequited and illicit love. As Heian fiction dealt largely with the aristocratic class for whose consumption it was written, so that of the Tokugawa period concerned the lives of the merchant class that read it. Ibara Saikaku (1642–93) wrote the most highly esteemed novels of the period, colloquial, poetic, and flavorful.

MODERN DEVELOPMENTS

The enormous range of Western literature first came to the attention of the Japanese late in the nineteenth century and inspired countless imitations of almost every one of its varieties. Adaptation of European naturalistic drama to Japanese themes involved a violent wrenching away from the conventions to which the Japanese were accustomed in their own theater. Similarly, the evolution of types of fiction that would simultaneously satisfy the public's old taste for the evocative and its new demand for complex and sustained narratives dealing with psychological and social themes has not been easy. The Meiji period was one of experimentation; one immediate problem was the substitution of natural, colloquial language for the archaic literary style that prevailed in formal writing. The recurring themes of Meiji novels are Japan's destiny in the world, the acceptance of new standards of social justice, and the fierce struggle in the minds of Japanese intellectuals between the old ways of the East and the new ones of the West. Futabatei Shimei was an early realist among Meiji novelists, creating almost plotless psychological descriptions of life in the upper middle class, which was most touched by westernization. Higuchi Ichiyô, the foremost woman writer of modern Japan, wrote realistic short stories subtly suggesting the difficulties of psychological adjustment to the greater fluidity of Meiji society.

In the years immediately following the turn of the century, a number of younger Japanese novelists struck out in reaction to the mid-Meiji predisposition to crudely realistic treatments of social and political issues. Shimazaki Tôson wrote natural istic problem novels of society, but the problems were presented in intimate psychological terms, and psychology became and remained the center of interest in Japanese fiction. Natsume Sôseki, writing between 1905 and 1914, used a variety of styles: realistic, as in *Kokoro,* a tragic story of an intellectual forced by his own devotion to everyday obligations into a pointless and thwarted life; satiric, as in *Wagahai wa Neko de Aru* (I Am a Cat), whose feline narrator pokes fun at human ways; and casually poetic, as in *Kusa-makura,* a fictional travel diary in the manner of the informal prose works of the Heian period. Mori Ôgai, an army surgeon for whom fiction was an avocation, examined psychological—particularly sexual—behavior from the background of his scientific training and attempted to counteract the current tendency in fiction of overemphasizing the importance of romantic love.

The bitterly satiric short-story writer, Akutagawa Ryûnosuke, killed himself in 1927 when he was still a young man. He left a number of sardonic masterpieces similar in some respects to the allegories of his Czech contemporary, Franz Kafka. *Kappa* is a mock-utopian description of a society of super-rationalistic river-dwarfs carrying to their logical absurdity the materialistic tendencies that Akutagawa feared in his own society. *Yabu no Naka* (In a Grove), on which the recent motion picture *Rashômon* was based, by juxtaposing several accounts of the same murder, examined human claims to noble, unselfish action and found them to be hypocritical.

An idealistic school of which Mushakôji Saneatsu is a typical member has continued to apply the methods of past psychological fiction to situations illustrative of man's moral nature, feeling that the foremost duty of fiction is to point out the fundamental human obligation of sympathy.

An important development of recent decades has been the revival of some of the styles of classic Japanese prose, emphasizing their refinement of language and qualities of evanescent, sensuous beauty. Tanizaki Jun'ichirô has translated the *Genji Monogatari* into modern Japanese and tries in his own fiction to emulate Lady Murasaki's evocation of a serene and self-sufficient world. The westernized protagonist of one of Tanizaki's novels cultivates ancient Japanese music and fine arts in a forlorn attempt to escape the feverishness of twentieth-century urban life. In reaction to a spate of novels of social and moral significance, he takes an amoral attitude toward life, finding aesthetic satisfaction in behavior that other writers could only find morally repugnant.

Postwar fiction cannot be easily summarized. Its most striking product is Tanizaki's *Sasame-Yuki* (Snowflakes), a vast and rambling tale of upper middle-class family life in prewar Osaka. Its great popularity is probably an index of the current need for escape from grim postwar realities, though other novelists continue to treat problems of current importance.

READINGS

Akutagawa, Ryûnosuke. *Rashômon, and Other Stories*. Translated by Takashi Kojima. New York, Liveright, 1952.

Aston, W. G. *A History of Japanese Literature*. "Short Histories of the Literature of the World." London, Appleton-Century, 1933.

Bowers, Faubion. *Japanese Theatre*. Foreword by Joshua Logan. New York, Hermitage, 1952.

Keene, Donald. *Japanese Literature; an Introduction for Western Readers*. London, John Murray, 1953.

Kobayashi, Nobuko (trans.). *The Sketch-book of the Lady Sei Shônagon*. New York, Dutton, 1930.

Kokusai Bunka Shinkokai (ed.). *Introduction to Classic Japanese Literature*. Tokyo, 1948.

Natsume, Sôseki. *Kokoro*. Translated by Ineko Satô. Tokyo, Hokuseidô, 1941.

Nippon Gakujutsu Shinkôkai. *The Manyôshû*. One Thousand Poems Selected and Translated from the Japanese. Tokyo, Iwanami, 1940.

Tanizaki, Jun'ichirô. *Ashikari and the Story of Shunkin*. Translated by Roy Humpherson and Hajime Okita. Tokyo, Hokuseidô, 1936.

Waley, Arthur. *Japanese Poetry, the "Uta."* Oxford, Clarendon Press, 1919; lithoprint ed., London, Lund Humphries, 1945.

Waley, Arthur (trans.). *The Tale of Genji*. New York, Literary Guild, 1935.

RELIGION AND PHILOSOPHY

Until recent times philosophy in Japan has been associated with one or other of the country's great religions. One cause, or perhaps effect, of this feature was that the energies of most Japanese with speculative turns of mind have always been devoted to the solution of practical problems of individual or social morality. As in the West, it has been felt that these interests were best served within the framework of an organized cult. Of Japan's three major faiths, one is native and the other two borrowed. The roots of modern Shinto may be found in the ritual practices of the primitive Japanese people. Buddhism originated in India but arrived in Japan from China and Korea in the sixth century of the Christian era. Confucianism was known to the Japanese from the earliest days of their intercourse with China but attained its greatest prestige in Japan only after about 1600. A fourth great religion, Christianity, came to Japan in the sixteenth century, was suppressed by the authorities from the seventeenth to the nineteenth, and acquired additional importance from the latter time on as one of the bearers of Western civilization.

Of all religions Buddhism occupies by far the most important place in the religious life of Japan. Its influence on the fine arts and on social institutions, which cannot be overemphasized, is described elsewhere in the present handbook. Japanese Buddhism shares its most important doctrinal features with the Buddhist faith in other parts of Asia. Those which serve to differentiate the religion from, for example, Christianity may be suggested from the following points of doctrine:

1. Buddhism is not theistic: it conceives of no supreme intelligence which created the universe and directs the affairs of man. Whatever absolute entity Buddhism recognizes comprises the universe as a whole, which is self-creating.

2. Buddhist ethics demand as the first human obligation sympathy for all beings. This sympathy should not be reserved solely for other men nor even for all other sentient beings but belongs properly to the entire universe, inanimate as well as animate.

3. The phenomena of the material universe are, to Buddhists, unreal, since they exist only relative to each other and limited by time. Attachment to things, therefore, is evil and the source of all suffering. Buddhist practices aim at freeing men from their earthly desires and preparing them by intellectual, psychological, or mystic means for "loss of self," that is, absorption into the undifferentiated real universe, independent of time and space. This loss of self is known as *nirvana,* or "extinction," and is the Buddhist salvation.

Though Buddhist philosophy is highly metaphysical and recondite, the popularity of the faith in Japan depended on the appeal of some of its other features. Some sects (for example, the Shingon and Tendai sects that flourished from the Heian era) emphasized ritualistic or magical means to salvation. A group of sects (Jôdo, Shin, and Ji) took as one of their principal objects of worship the supernatural being Amida, who deferred his own salvation in order to aid that of the rest of the suffering world. The Amidist sects thus appealed for popular support to the notion that salvation could be attained by dependence on the aid freely given by Amida. The Zen sect deprecated the efficacy of intellectual and contemplative means to salvation, insisting instead that enlightenment must come suddenly and might even be facilitated by an active life.

Japan's only native sect was that founded in the thirteenth century by Nichiren, who identified the salvation of the individual with the establishment of a Buddhist state and society. Unlike other Japanese sects, that of Nichiren is both nationalistic and intolerant of all other religions.

Since the Middle Ages Japanese Buddhism has undergone little doctrinal growth, and there has been considerable decline in the power and vitality of the faith as a whole. Still, nearly two thirds of the population are at least nominally Buddhist.

CONFUCIANISM

The Confucian cult in China incorporated many of the features of the primitive tribal religion of the Chinese people. To these ritualistic elements centuries of thinkers added complex metaphysical and ethical doctrines, the end product being closer to the Western idea of a philosophic school than to that of a religion. Confucian social and political doctrines formed the

theoretical basis for the Chinese state from about the time of
Christ; they provided the justification for absolute Imperial
rule and administration by a scholar class chosen on the basis of
talent. They even allowed the right of revolution in case the
sovereign should fail in his duties to the society. In theory some
of these political notions underlay the conduct of Japanese
government from the Heian period on, though they probably
had little influence on its actual practice. Confucian ideas as to
individual relationships in the family or in society had greater
vitality in Japan. One idea that the Japanese made peculiarly
their own was the emphasis on personal loyalty of servant to
master or of subject to sovereign as transcending all other
obligations. It was this mutual and unequal relationship tend-
ing to bolster the foundation of the state that appealed especially
to Japanese rulers in Tokugawa times and made of Confucianism virtually the official cult. Administrators of government,
both in the *Bakufu* and in the fiefs, were usually scholars trained
in classical Chinese learning. Education of the aristocracy was
the province of Confucian academies supported privately by
leading philosophers or at the expense of the feudal governments. Several schools flourished at the time, the principal of
which were as follows:

1. The *Bakufu's* own official school, descending from the
rationalistic Chinese school of Chu Hsi that dated from the
twelfth century.

2. A school emphasizing personal, rather than political, ethics
dating from the Ming scholar Wang Yang-ming (1472–1529).

3. The Ancient Texts School of Ogyû Sorai (1666–1728),
which stressed the need for sound scholarship in the funda-

mental Confucian writings in order to detect and throw out the accretions of later commentators.

4. Schools of economic thinkers, generally employed by feudal rulers to help solve pressing current problems. Confucians of this type such as Arai Hakuseki (1656–1726) and Dazai Shundai (1680–1747) contributed much to Japanese knowledge of the workings of finance, exchange, and distribution.

5. A school of Confucian nationalists founded by Yamaga Sokô (1622–85), who attempted to merge Confucianism with aspects of the native cult, founding the code of military virtue known as *Bushidô*.

6. Another nationalistic school sponsored by the princes of Mito, who belonged to a collateral branch of the Tokugawa family. Unlike Yamaga Sokô, these scholars remained in the fold of orthodox Confucianism but applied the theories of the Chinese state cult to the Japanese Imperial dynasty.

Confucianism as a genuine religious sect is no longer of any importance in Japan, though the contributions of three hundred years of thinkers in the Confucian philosophic tradition remain an important strand in the thought of our own time.

SHINTO

Primitive Japanese religion was animistic, conceiving of supernatural beings controlling all the forces of nature and dwelling in all natural things. Propitiating evil spirits and expressing gratitude to good ones were the principal functions of worship, and the cult had no sacred texts and no formulated articles of faith. It was not until Buddhism came on the scene that people began to call the native cult Shinto, "The Way of the Gods," for up to that time there had been no need to distinguish it from any other faith.

Contacts between Buddhism and Shinto modified both religions. As the Buddhist faith is not as a rule intolerant of other cults, it was possible to explain Shinto divinities as merely spirits of the Buddhist pantheon and Shinto ritualistic practices as permissible means to enlightenment. In this way the idea became accepted by some thinkers that the two faiths were simply different ways of expressing the same truth. Occasionally single temples would be built as houses of worship for both religions, just as elaborate dogmas were sometimes worked out to reconcile the apparent inconsistencies between them. This curious symbiosis between the two cults was known as *ryōbu-Shintō,* or dual Shinto. It is illustrative of the point of view Japanese take toward religion that they see no inconsistency in the same individual's embracing the tenets of two quite different faiths.

In time new Shinto sects sprang up that were not openly associated with any foreign religion. Most, however, bore marks of Japan's association with Buddhism, Confucianism, and, in the past hundred years, Christianity. Increased nationalistic feeling during the Tokugawa period stimulated close study of native institutions and the indigenous parts of the national character. Though some of this thought fitted into the scheme of one or another of the Confucian schools, an important group of thinkers of the eighteenth and early nineteenth centuries led a movement back to the un-sinicized native faith. Chief among them were Kamo Mabuchi (1697–1769), Motoori Norinaga (1730–1801), and Hirata Atsutane (1776–1843). The Meiji government recognized pure Shinto as the official state religion, even demanding certain ritual observances of devout adherents to other religions. In an attempt to dissociate Shinto from Buddhism, the government forced temples of the *ryôbu-Shintô* persuasion to declare unequivocally whether they were thenceforth to be considered Buddhist or Shinto. State Shinto was in many respects a political, rather than a religious, development, since it was officially cultivated by the government as a spur to patriotic and nationalistic feeling. Emperor worship was one of its features, as was the propagation of doctrines of expansionism and national self-determination. The Emperor himself symbolized the disestablishment of Shinto in 1946 by publicly denying his own divinity. Yet most Japanese could truthfully say at that time that they had never considered the Emperor a god in any Western sense. He was thought to be divine in terms of the primitive polytheistic cult of the Japanese people —a cult that saw divinity in all the manifestations of nature and society.

The Shinto sects were not abolished under the Allied occupation. Disestablishment simply meant that certain old state-supported shrines lost their government subsidization and were placed in the same legal position as the institutions of any other religion. Even Japanese Buddhists and some Christians still include observation of Shinto practices as part of their religious life.

CHRISTIANITY

Until late in the nineteenth century Christianity to the Japanese meant, by and large, Roman Catholicism. Intimations of sectarianism within Christianity came to Japan as early as the sixteenth century, but the Protestants with whom the Japanese came into contact—mostly English and Dutch merchants—were not proselytizers and left little influence on the religious life of Japan. Small societies of Catholics in Kyushu survived centuries of persecution during the Tokugawa period and still remain there.

Catholic, Protestant, and Orthodox missionaries went to Japan in increasing numbers after 1859. Full religious freedom was given to Christians in 1889. Japanese Christians numbered about 300,000 in 1940 and had increased to 428,000 by 1950. About two thirds are Protestant. An attempt was made by Japanese Protestants during and after the war to reduce the sectarianism within their ranks. The Church of Christ in Japan is an amalgamated body representing several of the major Protestant sects in other countries, Lutherans and Episcopalians remaining the principal independent bodies.

READINGS

Anesaki, Masaharu. *History of Japanese Religion with Special Reference to the Social and Moral Life of the Nation.* London, Kegan Paul, 1930.

Holtom, Daniel Clarence. *National Faith of Japan; a Study in Modern Shintô.* London, Kegan Paul, 1938.